I like books from authors who have lived out what they've written. Bill Wiese's new book, *Recession-Proof Living*, is an investment to secure your financial future. Bill shows you how to position yourself for success by having the right heart, the right attitude, and the right perspective. The knowledge shared in this book is a result of years of trusting God, obeying His Word, and applying biblical principles in his own life, leading to success. Bill shares from his own personal experiences so that you can reap the benefits from the invaluable lessons he has learned.

—Jentezen Franklin
Senior Pastor, Free Chapel
New York Times best-selling author, *Fasting*

God only shows things to the people He knows He can trust, and I understand why God picked Bill Wiese and gave him the vision he shares in his first book. Bill is an honest man, and God knew He could trust Bill. I have known Bill and Annette Wiese for several years now and have witnessed how their lives and their godly lifestyle have led to prosperity.

In *Recession-Proof Living* are true stories of how Bill has applied God's Word to many different situations and seen them turn around. I highly recommend this book because it will help everyone who reads it achieve success and gain understanding about how God can work supernaturally in our lives. It is not a formula for success; it's living a lifestyle that develops godly character. The stories shared are humorous, informative, and enlightening to God's message. I know that as you read this book and apply these principles to your own life, you will begin to see your situation greatly improve.

—Dr. Norvel Hayes
Founder and President, Norvel Hayes Ministries
Founder, New Life Bible College and New Life Bible Church

In his book *Recession-Proof Living*, Bill Wiese explains how principles of integrity will ensure that we become winners in life. Bill proves without any shadow of doubt that dishonest shortcuts can never compete with doing what's right. If ever there was a time in our history that we needed to know how to recession-proof our living, it's today. This book is funny, gripping, captivating, and essential. As Bill shares his life's experiences, you will enjoy every minute and learn how easy it is to prosper in a world that is becoming more and more dishonest.

—THEO WOLMARANS, ThD, DD
FOUNDING PASTOR, CHRISTIAN FAMILY CHURCH INTERNATIONAL

Bill and Annette Wiese have taught these great truths at my church, impacting many lives. Bill's thirty-plus-year background in business and constant seeking after God's wisdom in his own life has resulted in nuggets of truth seldom seen today. Bill's life experiences shared in this book help us to succeed in troubled times.

—DOUG CHAMBERS
SENIOR PASTOR, FULL GOSPEL CHURCH
BELLFLOWER, CALIFORNIA

RECESSION-PROOF LIVING

BILL WIESE

CHARISMA
HOUSE

Most CHARISMA HOUSE BOOK GROUP products are available at special quantity discounts for bulk purchase for sales promotions, premiums, fund-raising, and educational needs. For details, write Charisma House Book Group, 600 Rinehart Road, Lake Mary, Florida 32746, or telephone (407) 333-0600.

RECESSION-PROOF LIVING by Bill Wiese
Published by FrontLine
Charisma Media/Charisma House Book Group
600 Rinehart Road
Lake Mary, Florida 32746
www.charismahouse.com

Unless otherwise noted, all Scripture quotations are from are from the King James Version of the Bible.

Scripture quotations marked AMP are from the Amplified Bible. Old Testament copyright © 1965, 1987 by the Zondervan Corporation. The Amplified New Testament copyright © 1954, 1958, 1987 by the Lockman Foundation. Used by permission.

Scripture quotations marked NKJV are from the New King James Version of the Bible. Copyright © 1979, 1980, 1982 by Thomas Nelson, Inc., publishers. Used by permission.

Scripture quotations marked NLT are from the Holy Bible, New Living Translation, copyright © 1996, 2004, 2007. Used by permission of Tyndale House Publishers, Inc., Wheaton, IL 60189. All rights reserved.

Scripture quotations marked TLB are from The Living Bible. Copyright © 1971. Used by permission of Tyndale House Publishers, Inc., Wheaton, IL 60189. All rights reserved.

Cover design by Justin Evans
Design Director: Bill Johnson

Visit the author's website at www.soulchoiceministries.com.

Library of Congress Cataloging-in-Publication Data:
Wiese, Bill.
  Recession-proof living / Bill Wiese.
    p. cm.
  Includes bibliographical references.
  ISBN 978-1-61638-478-4 (trade paper) -- ISBN 978-1-61638-632-0 (e-book) 1. Success--Religious aspects--Christianity. 2. Real estate agents--Religious life. 3. Wiese, Bill. I. Title.
  BV4598.3.W49 2011
  248.8'8--dc23

                              2011025600

11 12 13 14 15 — 9 8 7 6 5 4 3 2 1
Printed in the United States of America

DEDICATION

This book is dedicated to those who have a sincere desire to learn God's Word and value it as hidden treasure. Those who will approach Scripture with reverence and maintain a humble, teachable heart will surely discover His blessings. My desire is to demonstrate God's involvement in every area of our lives if we will simply obey His Word. May the readers herein see His goodness, as we have seen.

ACKNOWLEDGMENTS

I WOULD FIRST LIKE to thank the Lord, who has done so much for me over my life, and especially my forty-one years in knowing Him as a Christian. He has watched over my wife and me so faithfully and has taught us how to live successfully. His Word is precious to us. He has been so gracious to me, especially by giving me my beautiful wife, Annette. She is an exceptional woman, and I love her deeply. Her dedication to the Lord is exemplary. There would not have been the first book, *23 Minutes in Hell*, without her. Both our parents' prayers and hearts have been with us all the way. We love them dearly. Our pastors pray for us and have been so supportive along this journey. We love them and greatly value their friendship. There are many who pray for us and write us, and we so appreciate their kind words and prayers. We thank you all so very much.

CONTENTS

Introduction ix

Chapter 1 Rising Early for a Special Guest 1

Chapter 2 My Schooling Never Prepared Me for This! 5

Chapter 3 Strife Avoided—Success Achieved 19

Chapter 4 Spending Dollars to Save Integrity 25

Chapter 5 A Gift in Secret 35

Chapter 6 Ten Dollars Buys More Than a Hundred 41

Chapter 7 More Honesty, Less Flattery 57

Chapter 8 Determined, Not Desperate 61

Chapter 9 Committed, Not Compromised 67

Chapter 10 The Only Guarantee Against Failure 69

Chapter 11 A Pilot's Checklist 73

Chapter 12 Activate the Blessings in God's Word 87

Chapter 13 Passing the Tests of Life 103

Chapter 14 Wisdom—Do You Have It? 115

Chapter 15 God's Wisdom Revealed. 133

Chapter 16 The Power of Humility 143

Chapter 17 The Fear of God 159

Chapter 18 Life and Death Are Within Your Power 181

Chapter 19 The Bottom Line—a Synopsis 195

Chapter 20 The God Many Don't Know. 203

Appendix A:
Additional Verses: A Pilot's Checklist 213

Appendix B:
Additional Verses: Fear of the Lord 220

Notes 223

HI, MY NAME is Bill Wiese, and I am the author of the *New York Times* best seller *23 Minutes in Hell*. By writing this book, *Recession-Proof Living*, I am not in any way abandoning my priority to share my twenty-three minutes in hell experience. I have been speaking about this full-time around the world during the past five years and will continue. That mission is my life and will not change.

The reason for writing this book is to give people a glimpse into my life prior to my experience and including seven years beyond. These true stories show how a commitment to the Lord has led me to prosper despite many challenges. I hope you glean the little wisdom I have gained during my thirty-five-year real estate career and apply it to your life in order for you to succeed. The basis for it all is God's Word, and it will work for anyone, even during difficult economic periods.

This book is not simply about how to make money, but

rather, how to develop the character needed to succeed in any economic time.

I learned there is only one way to achieve success in all areas of life. Now I was not a millionaire, nor a financial genius, but just the average guy going to work with the average job. And I had my share of challenging circumstances...

For instance, what do you do if you have only $50 left to your name, you have the credit cards charged to a tune of $175,000, you are in a commission-based job only, and the current market is at a standstill? How do you still maintain your high credit score and get free from all that debt? The Bible taught me how.

What do you do if the IRS hits you with an additional $45,000 in taxes owed and says you have only two weeks to pay it? You have no money and no one to borrow it from. Is there a way to pay it off in those two weeks? I learned how and did it.

What do you do if a business associate steals $60,000 from you?

How do you respond, and how do you get it back without fighting or suing him? I learned how and did it.

What do you do if one of your clients believes you are responsible for something bad that happened to them, and they lie about you in your workplace? How do you respond? What can you do to cause them to see their error, apologize, and hire you again for a profitable venture? I learned how and did it.

What do you do when you're told "the deal's off," and you have only ten seconds left to possibly save it? I heard only one word from God, which I spoke, and it stopped the client from leaving and saved the transaction. How did I know what that one word was? Hearing one word from God will always cause you to prosper.

However, you can be financially successful yet destitute in

the more important areas of life. Receiving instruction from God in all areas of our life is what constitutes victorious living. It is about a lifetime commitment to a godly lifestyle, not a quick formula for success.

My wife, Annette, and I are living a very fulfilling life, and we know it is because we applied these biblical truths and put God first.

I encourage you to read these stories and gain insight into the God whose help we need to overcome today's challenges.

CHAPTER 1

RISING EARLY FOR
A SPECIAL GUEST

I USUALLY BEGIN MY day early, and this one particular day I rose even earlier to pray. During my prayer time, I heard God tell me, "Study all the facts and figures regarding the neighborhood you live in." I don't mean that I heard an audible voice, but a still, quiet voice from within. As a real estate broker, I had recently begun to market the homes in this particular area. Later that morning, I began the research to acquire these facts. By that afternoon, I had memorized all the information. Later that evening, I received a call from a homeowner who wanted to sell his property. He said that he wanted to interview me and then two other agents afterward. He would then make his decision and list his home with the agent of his choice. I told him that would be fine.

During the interview, he began asking a series of questions having to do with various facts and figures about the neighborhood.

He asked, "How many models of my home are there?"

I responded, "Forty-one."

He then asked, "How many have sold this year?"

I replied, "Four."

He continued, "How many last year?"

I said, "Seven."

"How many total models are there?"

"Six."

"How many total in the complex?"

"One hundred eighty-two."

He asked, "How many are there of the other five?"

I said, "Thirty-five model plan 303; thirty plan 300; twenty-seven plan 301; twenty-six plan 302; and twenty-three plan 304."

He then asked, "How many acres is the complex?"

I said, "Thirty-three."

"How many acres is our lake?"

"One and one-half."

He then shook his head as if in amazement and asked, "How could you remember so many figures?"

I said, "It's part of my job to know them." Of course, I just learned all of this information that very afternoon.

Then he said, "You got the job!"

He didn't bother to interview the other two agents. I listed the home, thanked him, and left. As I was walking away, a neighbor stopped me and asked me if I had any homes for sale of a model like theirs. They were having dinner with some friends, and the friends liked their home. They went out for a walk to see if there were any for sale signs up, and they saw me. I told them I just listed one thirty seconds ago. They asked if they could see it. I turned around and went right back and knocked on his door. I asked him if I could show it to this couple. He said, "You certainly do work fast." We came in, looked at the home, and they bought it right then. It was the quickest sale I ever made. My commission was $15,000.

What if I didn't get up that morning to pray and had not heard God's voice? Since the seller asked all those questions, do you think I would have been given the listing if I couldn't have answered them?

God is always looking for ways to help and bless us. Since He comes by every morning, I want to be there to hear what He has to say. Job 7:17–18 states, "What is man, that thou shouldest magnify him?…and that thou shouldest visit him *every morning…*" (emphasis added).

> Those that seek me *early* shall find Me. Riches and honour are with me.
> —PROVERBS 8:17–18

> And in the morning came the word of the LORD unto me…
> —EZEKIEL 12:8

For further study, read: Deuteronomy 6:6–9; Job 1:5; Psalms 57:8–9; 59:16; 63:1; 78:34; 90:14; 108:2; 127:2; Proverbs 3:24; 8:17; 10:22; 27:14; Isaiah 6:8; 26:9; 42:6; Jeremiah 7:13; 25:3; 31:26; 32:33; Mark 1:35; 16:9; John 8:2; Acts 5:21.

CHAPTER 2

MY SCHOOLING NEVER PREPARED ME FOR THIS!

MY CLIENTS AND I arrived at the bank as scheduled at 9:00 a.m. in order to sign the loan documents. They were an elderly couple, and the husband was a paraplegic and rode in a wheelchair. We were taken to an office that sided to a large, open room with approximately thirty people at their desks. The loan processor approached us with a tall stack of papers to be signed by my clients, the buyers.

To give you a little background on this couple, the woman was extremely difficult. She had two completely separate personalities. Later I had discovered that she had been diagnosed as a schizophrenic. About halfway through the escrow, her daughter had told me that her mother was so impossible to even be around, that she was going to move away from the neighborhood now that her mother was moving in! She strongly declared to me that she couldn't live that close else her mother would drive her crazy!

However, her mother, my client, really liked me, and we got along just fine for the most part. There were times when she became another person and would flair up suddenly, becoming completely hostile and act insane for no apparent reason.

One particular time, just prior to this appointment to sign the loan documents, she showed up unannounced at my front door. Carrying her little dog, she just walked right in, put the dog down, and started swinging at me with arms flailing wildly and kicking at my legs. She had a large bracelet on her wrist, and, as she swung at me, I blocked it with my arm. The bracelet scraped down my arm, slicing open both my shirtsleeve and my arm. My white dress shirt was soon soaked with blood.

I had a stack of files on my desk, and in one swoop, she knocked them all on the floor, scattering papers everywhere. About this time, my wife's Yorkshire terrier came around the corner, and the two dogs were fighting and barking. The woman was screaming hysterically, and I was attempting to get her out of my house. She then threw her shoes at me, while kicking continuously. I tried to grab her arm and escort her out, but she was violent with her arms swinging in the air. Blood was now running down my arm, and at that moment, my next prospective buyer was approaching the door. They looked at me, startled and amazed. Keep in mind that I had never met these people before, and they now see the blood, torn shirt, fighting dogs, papers scattered on the floor, and me throwing an elderly lady out the door. This was not exactly a good first impression. I finally got her out, picked up her shoes, and threw them out the door. I proceeded to try and explain the situation to this potential buyer. You can imagine!

During the escrow, there were several other incidences similar to this one with this woman. One night I received a call from the police department. They said she had tried to unhook all the tubes in her husband at the hospital and take him out. The police came at the hospital's request, and she began kicking the policeman and hitting him. So they locked her up in the local jail.

You might be wondering, "Why didn't I cancel this sale?" Well, she insisted on continuing with the purchase, and the seller also wanted this to close, as they had already purchased another home. They were really counting on this sale, as their purchase was contingent upon their home closing.

One more important side note: the seller (the elderly couple's seller) had, on his own initiative, gained access to the home he was purchasing and just moved in during an afternoon. He had no permission and no agreement to do this. It had not closed escrow, there was nothing signed, and his seller didn't even know about his moving in. He moved in when some workers were there doing some repairs. The home was vacant, but you don't just move in before closing, especially without permission. I was responsible, as I was his agent also. I was handling both transactions. If the seller found out, there would be a big problem. This buyer was a very forceful man who just did whatever he wanted to do. I told him he must vacate immediately, and he simply refused. I continued to attempt to get him out, but since I was not the owner, there was little I could do. His seller was out of the country, so I couldn't reach her to discuss the matter. Looking back, that was a good thing.

So this was a mess, and all hinging on this one crazy lady! If she didn't close, then he couldn't either, and when the seller returned from out of the country, I would have had some serious explaining to do (as Ricky would say to Lucy). I just needed this to close, and then the problem would go away.

Back to the bank: we were all sitting in the bank president's office, which opened to the large office of about thirty working staff. The husband was paralyzed, so he couldn't sign anything. His name would be on title, but he only had to put an "X" on one form. As the wife began signing the stack of forms, she kept questioning if her husband was on title, since he wasn't signing. We explained that he was but that he didn't need to sign, because of his condition. After signing only two forms, she suddenly jumped up and tore the documents in pieces, claiming that we are all lying to her and that her husband wasn't on title. We explained again and showed her the form that showed that he was on title. Finally she sat down. They had to reprint the documents again, sign, and continue on. After two or three more papers signed, she again jumped up with the same scenario. We explained again, but this time she wouldn't listen. The entire office was now attentive and aware of what I was dealing with. She was very loud and boisterous.

I asked her to sit down, so she could read the form that explained in detail her husband's exemption. Finally convinced, she continued signing. Well, this scenario repeated about twenty-five times, not exaggerating. It was now approximately 4:00 p.m. Everyone was so tired of her outbursts. However, they were unaware that I had to get this accomplished because the seller had already moved into the house.

Another form to sign, and this time she got up to leave, and words would not convince her to continue. I prayed silently asking

God what to do next. I felt He impressed me to simply grab her hand gently, asking nicely and assuring her that things would be OK. It worked; she softened, sat down, and continued. We only had a few more forms to go. This went on two more times. This time the president of the bank came in to try to calm her down and help her understand. She began pounding on his chest saying, "Get out. Get out of this office, and leave me alone!" He said, "Lady, it is my office you're throwing me out of."

She stopped hitting him and then sat down. We all convinced her to continue. Then finally, with only one form to go, she gets up to leave. She says, "No more words, you will not convince me that he is on title. You all think he is dead already." I replied, "No, we don't." It didn't matter what we all said; she was heading out the door toward the elevator.

Virtually every person in that office had stopped working and was all looking at her as she pushed the button for the elevator. Everyone knew that after all this it would be such a waste to have it all fall apart with only one paper to go. I stood up and called to her, asking her to please listen, but she said, "No, leave me alone. I'm leaving!" I repeated, "Please listen to us. He *is* on title." She said, "Absolutely not. I'm finished."

I knew I had only seconds to convince her to stay, as the elevator was on its way up. But what could I possibly say now? She was truly finished. I quickly prayed under my breath asking the Lord to give me some answer. Suddenly, I heard a small voice inside say, "Checkbook." I thought, "What about a checkbook?" I didn't know why, but I felt impressed to tell her to pull out her checkbook. Why would I tell her that? I didn't know yet. I only had seconds, so I yelled out across the large office. I said, "Martha [name changed for privacy reasons], take out your checkbook right now!"

She stopped and said, "What? Why?" I said, "Just do it." I didn't know myself. All were now wondering what I was up to. Everyone had stopped their work and watched. Just then, the elevator doors opened. She started to get in but then turned toward me and let the doors close. She didn't get on it.

She again said, "What does my checkbook have to do with this?"

Suddenly, I got the word *analogy* in my mind. Then, I got it! I understood. You see, she didn't believe her husband was on title because he wasn't signing anything. So I said to her, "Martha, is your husband's name on your checkbook?" I was hoping the answer would be no for the analogy to make sense.

She said, "No, it is not."

"Thank God," I thought! I then questioned her, "But is his name on the account at the bank?" Hoping it was! I asked her, "Can he withdraw the money just as you can?"

She said, "Well, yes, all our accounts are in both names."

I said, "But his name is not on your checkbook, yet his name is on the account."

Then she got it. She could see that he could be on the account, yet have her name only on her own checkbook.

I said, "Just the same way, his name is on the title but not showing on the paperwork."

She saw it and said, "Oh, all right then, I'll sign the papers."

The analogy caused her to finally understand. She signed the last page. Thank God! With a sigh of relief, the entire bank staff stood up and applauded. The bank president approached me, shook my hand, and offered me a position at the bank! I laughed and thanked him.

My point is, if I didn't pray and hear that quiet, small voice say, "Pull out your checkbook," I would not have been able to save this whole transaction. Would you have thought of that? No, and neither would I. All parties were benefited, success achieved, and the escrows closed.

God teaches us how to be successful if we will listen. I can't tell you what a relief that was for me, and actually, for all the people at the bank. God came through again all the way. The Bible tells us in John 10:27, Jesus said, "My sheep hear my voice, and I know them, and they follow me." In Luke 12:12, Jesus said again, "For the Holy Ghost shall teach you in the same hour what ye ought to say."

Proverbs 16:1 says, "The preparations of the heart in man, and the answer of the tongue, is from the LORD."

I am the LORD thy God which teacheth thee to profit.
—ISAIAH 48:17

Becoming All Things to All People

I had a property for sale that was in a poor location in the community. It backed up to a busy street. The noise was too much for most people. I had a call one day from some people out of state that used to live in California. They wanted a two-bedroom home in their old neighborhood, which happened to be the same as where I resided. I told them about this property I had for sale. It turned out to be the very same home they used to rent three years earlier. That was extremely remote to have the very same property for sale that they used to rent! They agreed to purchase it, sight unseen, since they were very familiar with the home already. They seemed to be a very pleasant couple.

After approximately three weeks into the escrow, the husband began saying some very strange things on occasion. Now the seller of this home had already purchased his new home, which was contingent on this home closing. However, the contract didn't state that important fact. It was written up that it was noncontingent, which left him in a terrible position. He was now obligated to close, even if this transaction fell out. Needless to say, he was very anxious to get this transaction closed.

Our buyer, we'll call him "John," started becoming aggravated with every little thing. We had a property inspection done, and many of the minor items on the report became "major" to him—the largest item being, the air conditioner didn't cool as much as it should. I explained we would have an A/C specialist come and repair it. He suddenly went ballistic and started yelling over the phone in an insistent, loud, dramatic voice.

He said, "Bill, those people don't know anything. I have to do everything myself. I'm the only one who knows what to do. I must be there. I'll fly out and come to the rescue. Are you with me, Bill, are you with me?" I replied, "Yes, John, I'm with you." He continued, "I can't hear you, Bill, say it louder." Again I said, "I'm with you, John, I'm with you." "You're not saying it with fire in your voice, Bill; say it like you mean it, say it loud." Now I'm shouting over the phone, "I'm with you! I'm with you!" "All right now, Bill, that's the spirit!" John declared. My wife would hear me shouting in a dramatic tone and wonder what was going on. This went on daily, several times a day for a week.

Then he flew out to see the A/C guy and do all inspections himself. The home had a trash compactor, and he thought it was too noisy. So he opened his briefcase and pulled out a decibel rating meter device that will read the amount of decibels the appliance outputs. I couldn't believe he had one! He opened his jacket, and the inside was lined with screwdrivers and other small tools.

He then said, "Bill, this A/C man doesn't know anything. We must go up on the roof (where the compressor sat) and check it out ourselves." He didn't believe anyone was capable except himself. He would get in my face and scream at me like a military sergeant and say, "I can't hear you, Bill. Are you with me?"

"Yes, I'm with you."

"I can't hear you. Say it with passion and like you mean it, Bill."

"I'm with you, John. I'm with you."

I would have to go through this routine daily, and my voice was getting hoarse. It was ridiculous! And this is not exaggerated but understated. I couldn't wait for this to finally close escrow so I could get my voice back—and more.

We would be standing out in front of the home on the sidewalk, and he would be screaming at me, "I can't hear you, Bill!" And I would have to scream it back over and over. Finally, he flew back to Texas with a couple of weeks to go before it closed. From Texas he calls one day and says, "I'm tired of having to do everything myself. No one is capable but me."

This was not the case, of course, and everything was already worked out. But in his mind there was so much more to do. Just like the noise decibels, there were little things that he felt were not perfect, and the house had to be perfect. The few items left were really minor, such as one electrical wall plate was cracked. A new one cost about $1.39. I told him I would fix those items myself.

His reply was, "I'm canceling escrow and backing out."

Now, at this point, he was obligated to close, as all the inspections and other periods had passed. He was under contract, and the seller could sue him or at least keep his deposit money. I explained that to him, but it didn't matter. He was worried about the electrical plate and an outside faucet that had an occasional drip. I told him I would pay for the small repairs and get them fixed. He said, "No, it's the principle." So he hung up and called the escrow company to cancel.

I thought, "How do I get him to continue?" He was definitely obligated to perform at this point, as it had been two months. The loan was approved, and all major repairs were completed. The seller was really counting on this in order to close his purchase. I prayed with my wife, and I felt impressed not to fight him but to join him. I called him back after two days had passed and said, "John, I can't believe you are quitting on me. I need you to help me with these final repairs, and now you're not with me. I need to hear you say, 'I'm with you, Bill! I'm with you!' And say it loud, like you mean it. Now come on and get yourself together. You and I can do it together. Are you with me, John! Are you with me!"

I shouted it with passion, and suddenly he jumped in, "I'm with you, Bill! I'll come to the rescue. Don't worry. I'll fly out tomorrow." And he did! I went up on the roof with him, we checked out everything, and all was fine. I was the one shouting at him now, and he stayed with me.

The property closed escrow, and they loved the home. They lived there for seven years. Then they wanted a larger house, so they called me to sell it.

You might say, "Well, Bill, that was manipulation. How is that godly?" Yes, in a sense, it was manipulation. But I was only attempting to get him to fulfill his contractual obligation, do what's right, and avoid losing his deposit and/or a lawsuit. He was the one in default, and by this time, it would have caused the seller some damages.

They ended up happy and loved the home, as they would testify. And when they wanted to sell and move, I did sell it, and I helped get them happily moved. This time he didn't do all that yelling. He had accepted the Lord into his life, because I had shared with him about Jesus. God can heal any person.

Scripture says in 1 Corinthians 9:22, "To the weak became I as weak, that I might gain the weak: I am made all things to all men, that I might by all means save some." Now that verse is in regard to salvation, but if it will work for that, it will work for anything. I needed to act as he did in order for him to get back in the game, and for him to stop exaggerating the small repairs. I believe at times like this, we need to have the wisdom of God. If you see it as deceit, then I think you missed the point. It was the right thing to do to guide him in keeping his contractual obligation. I knew they loved the home and would be happy, and they were. He simply needed a nudge to continue. Also, he did accept the Lord as his Savior and become a Christian. He is much better today and communicates clearly and rationally. There is no more yelling or dramatics, as his mind is healthier and clear. We are also on very good terms together and still speak to this day. As a matter of fact, he recently called me to move again. God worked it out for good to all parties involved. Proverbs 3:5–6 states, "Trust in the LORD with all thine heart; and lean not unto thine own understanding. In all thy ways acknowledge him, and he shall direct thy paths."

PS: It took about a week to get my voice back from all that yelling!

Power in a Handkerchief—Knowing the Right Strategy

I had a call from a man who wanted to list his home that was located in the area I worked and lived. He explained that his wife, who was also on title, had just been released from a mental institution. He told me that she was still extremely difficult to communicate with and that it would be nearly impossible to get her to sign any papers. I set the appointment and went to their home. She was quite odd and very temperamental. However, she signed the listing agreement. I left, and as soon as I walked out the door, she began screaming; throwing glasses, pots, and pans; and going absolutely wild. The husband came outside and told me that this was her normal behavior. He commented that it would be a miracle if she signed the sale contract when one was received.

I came over the next day to show the house to an elderly woman. We knocked, and no one answered. I proceeded to open the door, since he had given me a key, and suddenly the woman came around the corner. At first she was a bit riled, but she said to come in. We were walking through the home, and all of a sudden she started screaming and throwing things. My elderly client was afraid and locked herself in the bathroom. The lady started turning over the furniture, pulling the china cabinet over, and so forth. I managed to get the elderly woman out of the bathroom. I was holding her hand, guiding her out of the house hurriedly when the woman started throwing things from off the coffee table at us. I shielded the elderly woman as glasses, ashtrays, plates, and so on were hitting my back, blocking them from hitting my client.

We finally made it out the door, my client crying, scared and upset—to say the least. She loved the home but was too afraid to buy it and deal with this crazy lady. I explained to her that I would handle everything, and she wouldn't need to get involved. We wrote up a full price offer.

I felt, at this point, that I would need special prayer to get these papers signed by this obviously emotionally disturbed woman. I called my pastor at that time and told him the situation. He said he would pray over a handkerchief, anoint it with oil, and that I should place the handkerchief in my pocket and bring it to the meeting. He said and prayed that the anointing oil, which represented the Holy Spirit, would take authority over those demonic spirits in the woman when I came into her home. (See Acts 19:12.)

Well, we made the appointment. I came up to the door, and I heard her screaming, throwing things, and being out of control. I knocked, but she was so loud, no one heard me. I then just opened the door and let myself in. She was yelling, and suddenly as I walked through the door, she became calm and looked at me and said, "Do you have some papers to sign?" I said, "Yes," and was surprised to see the obvious change. Her husband was completely in shock, as he had been seeing her in this violent state for weeks now. She said, "All right, let's sign them right now."

I placed the papers in front of her, and she started signing. She signed everything, then suddenly grabbed the papers and tore them in pieces. She had a momentary outburst. I had felt the Lord instruct me to bring an additional complete set of papers, so I pulled them out and said to her, "That's all right. I know selling can be emotional, so let's just try again." She calmed down and proceeded to sign them all. Praise God! I then got up, said goodbye, and walked out the door.

As soon as the door closed, she started up again and threw a glass and other items at the door. I heard glass breaking and thuds hitting the door as I was walking away. Her screams could be heard a block away.

She remained calm as long as I was in the house, just as my pastor prayed. Those demons couldn't manifest, because the Holy Spirit is far greater than those demonic spirits. (See 1 John 4:4.) I know this sounds too wild to be true. It does to me too, as I'm writing it. But I assure you, as truly as I live, this is not an exaggeration. I told my pastor the story after this all occurred. It happened exactly as I have told it.

We closed the sale, and the very next day the woman was found walking down the middle of the freeway in her nightgown at 2:00 a.m. Someone told me that this was in the newspaper. She was taken back to the mental institution.

It was amazing that she was let out, just long enough to complete the sale, as we needed her to sign. She was declared competent but then recommitted and declared incompetent after the transaction had closed. This was another sale that I wouldn't have made if I had not received the proper prayer for the authority over the devil. You might think that this story is crazy, but it happened, and God blessed me again with the sale.

> For thou, LORD, wilt bless the righteous; with favour
> wilt thou compass him as with a shield.
> —PSALM 5:12

CHAPTER 3

STRIFE AVOIDED— SUCCESS ACHIEVED

IN 1981 AND 1982, interest rates were at 19 percent, and the real estate market was at a standstill. There was a builder who had built this tract of homes and had thirty-three homes remaining unsold. He had then lost them in foreclosure. I was working at a large real estate company at the time but was just leaving to start my own business. Another agent at that office and I went to the bank that had the foreclosed homes. We asked them if they would consider selling one home at a time. They initially said no, as they wanted one buyer for all thirty-three properties. We then asked, "What if we could come up with at least half of the homes sold to individuals within thirty days? Would you then consider letting us sell all thirty-three to individuals?" They said they would consider it.

The other agent and I agreed that we would each contact our clients and try to write up as many contracts as we could in the next couple of weeks. We added a 6 percent fee to the prices the bank quoted us as the sales price. During that next two weeks, I wrote up fifteen offers, and he wrote up one or two. He then called the banker and made an appointment with him, unbeknownst to me. He told the banker he had sixteen or seventeen sold and asked if the bank would sign a listing agreement with his broker. They agreed and signed a 6 percent listing for each home. He then came to me and told me that he had gotten a listing signed and he was now going to take 3 percent of all my sales for himself. "You can't do that, as we had agreed to each get paid the 6 percent on each contract we each would write," I said.

"I don't care about what I said," he said. "I now have the listing signed in my name, and our broker will side with me, since I have now become friends with the banker."

He had been playing golf and establishing a rapport with the banker unbeknownst to me. At this point, the bank didn't even know that I was the one who wrote up all these contracts. Well, 3 percent of my commission was approximately sixty thousand dollars. This was a lot of money, and it was rightly mine. He said if I didn't sign a paper paying him my half, then they would take all of it and give me nothing. I was in a weak position, since the listing was not in my name, and right after we had started with this agreement, I had left the company and started on my own. I had gone to the broker and presented my case, but he felt more of an allegiance to the other agent and wouldn't do anything about it.

If I sued, it would take time, and my fifteen clients were excited about getting their new homes right away as they had made financial arrangements. Court would have dragged it on, and they were not in a position to wait. Right at this time, one of my buyers, who was a multimillionaire, came to me and said, "I will buy all thirty-three homes, and you can cut out the guy who is taking half your fee." I had shared the situation with him; he was also a friend. So at this point I had a choice. If I would have called the banker, I'm sure they would rather deal with only one buyer than thirty-three, as they had indicated in the beginning. Plus they would all be sold right then. I'm sure the banker would have negotiated with the other broker to get out of the listing, or found some way to be able to work with this one buyer who had cash for all thirty-three homes. My one buyer would then sell fourteen of the homes to my buyers, thereby honoring my contracts with them, and I would continue to sell all the remaining homes myself. It was a very difficult decision for me. I knew if I went with my one buyer, I would get into strife and possibly a lawsuit. The Bible says to avoid strife. If I didn't, I had to give away my sixty thousand dollars to a thief.

I decided not to go with my millionaire buyer. I signed over the sixty thousand dollars. That was not easy to do. He was so arrogant and could have cared less about our agreement. Here I had a chance to get back at this unscrupulous agent, but inside I felt that would be wrong. I would have made even more than the additional sixty thousand dollars, because I would have been able to sell all thirty-three homes.

Nevertheless, I felt a peace in my heart that I was doing the right thing. The Lord wanted me to trust Him and stay out of conflict (Prov. 3:5–6). Well, three weeks after I signed the paper, I had sold enough homes to earn another sixty thousand dollars. I didn't normally earn sixty thousand dollars in three weeks. It normally took six months at that time.

God blessed my business and gave it all back in that short time, all because I avoided strife. Strife is one of the worst things you can be involved in, and we are to avoid it like the plague. In addition, the Lord instructs us to immediately forgive the one who wrongs us. And I did. I didn't even feel any animosity toward him. As far as I was concerned, it never even happened. God gives you that kind of peace when you trust Him and do it His way.

> Let nothing be done through strife.
>
> —PHILIPPIANS 2:3

> For ye are yet carnal: for whereas there is among you envying, and strife…
>
> —1 CORINTHIANS 3:3

> It is an honour for a man to cease from strife.
>
> —PROVERBS 20:3

> A wrathful man stirreth up strife.
>
> —PROVERBS 15:18

> A froward man soweth strife.
>
> —PROVERBS 16:28

> To whom ye forgive anything…lest Satan should get an advantage of us.
>
> —2 CORINTHIANS 2:10–11

Plead my cause, O LORD, with them that strive with
me: fight against them that fight against me.

—PSALM 35:1

If we turn it over to God, He will fight our battles for us.

CHAPTER 4

SPENDING DOLLARS TO SAVE INTEGRITY

THERE WAS A season when I was so busy with real estate that I couldn't take on any more work. That, of course, is a good place to be. Well, someone called and wanted me to list their condominium. They insisted I handle it. They didn't want another agent. I then called a friend named Ike, who had his license but was going to Bible college at the time. He and his wife, Roxanne, were living on campus and really needed some money. I asked if he could help me market it and do half the work if I took the listing. I would give him half the fee, which represented a substantial amount. He said, "Yes, absolutely." I then went on the appointment to meet the people and list the property. As I was walking out the front door after just listing it, a car drove up and a man asked if I was a Realtor (I suppose I looked the part being in a suit). I said yes. He asked if I knew of any places for sale. I told him that I had just listed this property five minutes ago. He and his wife wanted to see it, so I knocked on the door. The owners were surprised to see me so fast with a buyer.

Well, the people loved it and bought it right then. Now I was faced with giving half of the commission to Ike. I had asked him if he would do the work of finding a buyer, and now there was no need. However, I didn't know that he really needed to pay off his college tuition to get his degree. He was really counting on it. I felt strongly inside to pay him the money anyway.

I realized, as I believe the Lord impressed me, that the reason the buyer came along so quickly was because Ike and Roxanne had been praying that God would supply their need. God blessed me with a quick sale for their sake. If I would have looked at it the way most would normally, I wouldn't have given him the money, and I would have failed a test. It would have been easy to have thought, "Well, God really wanted me to have the whole commission." The test was to see if I would keep my word and pay him the half. God blessed me with a quick sale, and if Ike wouldn't have agreed to help me, I wouldn't have even gone on the appointment to list the home. There would not have been even half of the commission for me to enjoy.

If we will not get greedy, God will bless us and all involved. The Bible says to keep your word, bless a brother, and treat others as you would want to be treated. It was a test for me, and they had their prayers answered. One of the keys to success is to recognize when God is testing us or when the enemy is trying to steal from us. The tests from God are always to see what is in our hearts (1 Sam. 16:7; 2 Chron. 32:31). Is there greed, or is there generosity?

Easy to Rationalize

There was an elderly couple who wanted to list their home with me. They had done some research to determine the sale price prior to my appointment with them. As we discussed the list price, they wanted to put it on the market at substantially lower than what I knew it would sell for. I told them the fair price, and they still said, "No, we want to price it low so we can move out fast, and we don't care if we lose some." I knew that it would still sell quickly if priced at the correct market value. And that price was approximately fifty thousand dollars higher than what they wanted. I told them again, and they still wanted it at the lower price. By the way, this is very rare. Most sellers overvalue their property.

Well, the thoughts went through my mind such as, "They are content with the lower price, so just list it and buy it yourself. They will be happy even at this lower price." However, would that be the right thing to do? Would I really be looking out for their best interest? I knew God would not be pleased if I hadn't looked out for them and insisted on the higher price. So I did list it higher and sold it within thirty days. Sometimes we can rationalize a situation to our benefit, but to show love and to "do unto others" will always be the right thing to do. We will reap what we sow.

> For the ways of man are before the eyes of the LORD,
> and he pondereth all his goings.
>
> —PROVERBS 5:21

Standing Up to Evil

I was showing a buyer some properties one day, and we ended up driving through a particular neighborhood he really wanted to reside in. We drove up and down the streets, because there was nothing on the MLS (multiple listing service), and there was only one "For Sale by Owner" sign. We stopped, and my client said, "I want to buy it. I am familiar with that floor plan, and I like the location." I said, "Don't you want to see what it's like inside?" He commented that it didn't matter, as he was going to completely remodel it anyway.

I went and knocked on the door, leaving the buyer in the car. The owner answered and invited me in. We talked a bit; he gave me the price and signed a one-party show agreement and agreed to let me show the home to my client. He then made a comment as I was about to walk out the door. He said, "Just don't show my home to a black man. I won't let a black man in the door."

I couldn't believe my ears. I thought that this kind of prejudice was long gone, or at least not in the big city. But it sure wasn't. Well, my buyer didn't need to see the property and was willing to purchase it sight unseen. I could have simply written up the offer, gotten it signed, and the seller would never know. Many times the buyer and seller never meet. This was at a time when I really needed the sale. However, I said to the seller, "I would never show your property, or sell it, if it was the last property on the earth. Prejudice is absolutely disgusting and completely wrong in God's sight and in the law's sight."

I walked out the door and got into the car. I proceeded to tell the buyer what had happened and that I wouldn't want him to buy that property if it was the last one on earth. He didn't care and wanted to buy it anyway, even though he was a black man.

I said, "No, please don't. Let's wait and find another one. I don't want that seller to have the pleasure of a quick, easy sale like this would be, and I do not want to deal with a person so warped as he is."

He said, "All right, we will wait for another."

Well, one week passed when another home came up, and it was in an even better location, lower price, and in better condition. God blessed the man's purchase. The other property sat there for one year before it sold.

This event, along with some others in my career, showed me the ugliness of prejudice and that it still sticks its twisted head up on occasion. We pray it continues to lessen.

Now, if I had let my flesh rule, I would have gone ahead with my client's wishes and written up the sale. I needed the money at the time, but it would have been wrong.

Standing up against evil is what was needed and not to just shrug it off and go about our business. If we would all stand up for what is right and condemn that which is evil, we would all live in a better world.

> And have no fellowship with the unfruitful works of darkness, but rather, reprove them.
> —EPHESIANS 5:11

> They that forsake the law praise the wicked: but such as keep the law contend with them.
> —PROVERBS 28:4

Acts 10:34 states that God is no respecter of persons. Our conscience also should guide us and tell us what is right and wrong, but many people have a seared conscience. Their hearts can deceive them (Prov. 28:26; Eccles. 9:3; Jer. 17:9), and that is why we must judge by the Word of God (2 Tim. 3:16). If we do it God's way, we, and those involved with us, will come out as winners.

It's Not Always About the Money!

I went into the real estate business in 1973 in Florida and became a broker. I decided to move to California and also received my real estate license there in 1977. I first worked for an independent company of about fifteen agents. Shortly after I went to work for this broker, he shared with me and another agent named Bob a dream that he had. He proceeded to tell us, "In this dream I was in my office, a new office, which was not the current one. It had all glass walls on two sides. Then, a storm hit the office and blew in all the glass. After the glass had been broken, a woman walked in and tried to seduce me (he was a married man). Secondly, a man approached me to offer me political power and position, but it required a donation and a compromise of ethics. Lastly, a young man came to me with a very fair business proposition that was good for me, but that I (the broker) turned him down and hurt the man financially. These were three tests in my life. That was the end of the dream." He was concerned that in the dream he had failed these tests. We told him the dream was a warning and to be on guard so he didn't have to fail the tests.

Well, one year later, he was moving the office to a new location. We (all the sales agents) came to work the day after moving into the new location, and here it was with two walls of all glass.

Bob and I looked at each other and remembered the dream the owner-broker had shared with us a year prior.

About three months had passed, and I was at home one day standing outside talking to my neighbor, and suddenly we heard this roar like a freight train approaching. We wondered, "What was that loud sound?" We looked across the open field and saw a tornado approaching. It was headed straight for us. It was not a large tornado such as you would see in Tornado Alley, but it still was substantial. We began praying, and all of a sudden the tornado rose up and passed over us. As we looked up, we were viewing the bottom of the tornado. It was like someone picked it up and carried it away.

Well, it touched down again and hit a building and blew in all the glass. No one was hurt, but all the glass had been broken in this office building in Santa Ana. Guess what building it hit? It was our new office that I worked in. It was the only damage that occurred from the tornado. As I recall, this was in the newspaper. The next day Bob and I again remembered the dream and said to each other, "What an accurate dream. This has actually happened." The broker remembered also and was astounded.

If the rest of the dream were to come true, then there would be three tests coming for the broker. At this point he should be on guard and not fail these tests, right? He should guard himself, as the dream was a warning to him. About six months had passed, and we noticed a young, very attractive woman come into the office and ask to see the broker. No one else thought anything about it, except for Bob and me. It turned out that he started seeing her and had an affair. There was test number one: failed, in spite of the warning. About a month later, a man came to the office and offered the broker a political position, but we found out that it was only given if a substantial donation would be given for some tainted agenda of the party. He took the position and gave the donation. Test two: failed.

Five or six months later, I was given an opportunity to work at a larger office, where you could keep 100 percent of the commission. A desk fee would be paid on a monthly basis regardless if you make a sale or not. It was the latest thing at that time, as it would attract the heavy hitters who earned more commission. I decided I would change offices and go. Bob did also. The last day of my employment there, I had an appointment to possibly list a house. Well, that evening the people wanted to see me, as I was referred by their friend. I explained to them that I would start the next day at my new office. It didn't matter to them one way or the other, as long as I would service the property.

I was faced with whether to have them sign the listing tonight or wait until tomorrow and list it with the new company. They were fine to wait until morning. If I listed it tomorrow, I would not have to split the commission as I would with my current broker. I was on a 70/30 split. He gets 30 percent of the fee when it sells. If I listed it tomorrow, I get 100 percent, and no split. So why not wait until tomorrow? I thought that this may be a test for myself to see if I would take the listing now and pay my broker the 30 percent and really leave on great terms. Perhaps I am to leave with blessing my broker. I decided to list it now, pay him the 30 percent but ask him if I could take the listing with me. He would still get his 30 percent and have no liability. I thought that I would go above and beyond.

There would be nothing wrong with waiting one day. I just wanted to leave on a good note, and paying him the 30 percent would show my intentions were good. There would be nothing left remotely in question.

The next morning, the day I was leaving, I went to him and told him the whole story. I asked if I could take the listing and still pay him his 30 percent. He would get paid and have no responsibility or liability, as I would take the listing under the new broker's name and cancel this one. He would have zero liability. This, I assumed, he would be very happy to do. Instead, he said, "No, I'll keep the listing, and I'm going to only pay you 30 percent, not your normal 70. I will get the 70 percent." Well, I was shocked. This was wrong and unethical. It was actually stealing. I explained that the people only listed it because they wanted me to be their agent, as I was highly recommended by their friends. They wanted the listing with me and not the company. He said, "No, I'm keeping the listing, and I'm not giving you more than 30 percent." I was shocked that he would be so greedy and insist on keeping the listing.

So there was test three, about being fair. I was amazed, not only because I was part of his three tests, but also because he failed to recognize all three tests of which he was warned about by God.

I had shared with the owners of the property as to my decision to first give the listing to my current broker. We talked a bit about the integrity that the Bible teaches and the characteristics a Christian should embrace. They were not Christians and were asking questions as we discussed the Bible. They commented that they were "refreshed" with my concern for another. I told them I would service them no matter if I were paid or not. Somehow I would handle it. Well, I did manage to service their listing, even though my old office had the property. I did all the showings and all the paperwork. They were happy. They had told me that they were impressed with my caring about my broker.

Several years later I saw them, and they wanted to tell me a story. They had gone to dinner shortly after the sale closed, and they were discussing religion with their friends. They all were not Christians but were talking about how a true Christian should keep his word and show concern for others. However, many they had met had not displayed those characteristics, especially when it came to money.

They shared with their friends that they had firsthand experience with a Christian who *did* show that kind of integrity. They ended up going to a local church that weekend, and the pastor was talking about honor, integrity, and going above and beyond as Christians. They ended up committing their lives to the Lord and became Christians. They wanted me to know that because I showed those qualities, it led them on that path and helped influence their decision. I was surprised and very excited with that outcome. It is nice to hear sometimes what happened with those whom we have planted seeds into. People do observe our actions, and we never know how we may affect them.

God's way is to warn people so they can avoid tragedy. Part of the broker's tests was also my test to see if I would not get greedy and then to forgive him. We all need to be quick to forgive, hold no animosity, respond with love, and move on. I'm not saying to be a doormat. We should voice truth, but as Jesus said in Matthew 5:40, "If any man will sue thee at the law, and take away thy coat, let him have thy cloak also." He also said to "love your enemies, bless them that curse you, do good to them that hate you" (v. 44). It is not always easy, but Jesus said to do it "that ye may be the children of your Father which is in heaven" (v. 45).

I've learned to always keep my eye on the goal! Keep in view the big picture. How would God judge my conduct?

CHAPTER 5

A GIFT IN SECRET

ONE EVENING, MY wife and I had three couples over to our home to celebrate one couple's anniversary. We lived in a small patio home, so the neighbor's home was in close proximity to our home. During the course of the evening, we were all talking and then the phone rang. It was our neighbor, an elderly couple, who called to complain about the noise. Well, we were not in any way loud, as I was very aware of our volume. It was only about 8:00 p.m. No one was talking loud, and there was no drinking going on. The elderly couple was not used to any noise at all, as we were always quiet, and it was a very quiet neighborhood. They were yelling at me over the phone and really angry for no reason.

I wanted to tell them a thing or two, but I refrained and told them we would be extra quiet.

The next day, I felt impressed to buy a flower arrangement for them. I took it over to them, and they were surprised. I simply wanted to show them kindness. They invited me in and then proceeded to tell me that they wanted to sell their home. I ended up listing it that evening! The following day I had a call from a well-known Christian artist, a singer, who wanted a home similar to the one I just listed. I took her over to see it, and she loved it. She bought it that day. I ended up listing and selling the property in two days and was paid a handsome amount. This was a sale I wouldn't have made if I had responded in the typical fashion. Proverbs 21:14 says, "A gift in secret pacifies anger [strife]" (NKJV). If we show kindness and understanding, we will always succeed.

Refuse to Be Offended

I had listed a property for sale that was in need of a complete remodel. I had found a nice couple who had purchased the home and planned on doing just that. However, they didn't know any contractors or how to go about it. I had decided to help them after the closing, since I knew all the people to do the work. I had done this for approximately fifty others in that same neighborhood, and the contractors were very familiar with the models and working with each other. I had never received compensation for this but simply wanted to help the people. Everyone in the neighborhood was very pleased with the outcome of their homes.

We started, and it had taken about five months to complete. The owners and I had become fairly well acquainted during that time. Finally, the home was finished, and it was beautiful. They were extremely happy. Well, about six months had passed, and my wife and I came home one night with a message on our recorder. It was them stating that they were so angry at me and never wanted to see my face again. They were speaking in a hateful tone and went on to say that their home had been vandalized. They said, "You are despicable for selling us a home in a neighborhood where homes get broken into. It is your fault this happened to us. We never want to see you again. You are despicable, and we are going to let everyone know how terrible you are."

Well, my wife and I were shocked. First of all, I lived a few doors away from them and had lived there for twenty years. It was a very good neighborhood and had one of the lowest crime rates in the city, according to the city police report. I immediately picked up the phone and called them. They proceeded to spew out more of the same. They felt it was my fault and that I was a terrible person for selling them a home in this terrible area. Their TV, computer, and some jewelry were stolen. I explained that I was so sorry to hear of their loss and understood the emotional pain they felt with such a violation.

I explained that it had always been an excellent area and had almost no crime in twenty years. I explained that the low crime rate was one of the reasons my wife and I lived there. I tried my best to convince them and console them, but they said, "Don't ever call us again. You disgust us," and then hung up.

Well, again, I was shocked, as we had become somewhat close, and I didn't think they were capable of that kind of anger and hatred for something so unjustifiable. I thought to myself, "After all I helped them with—and for free." I discussed with my wife what we should do. After we prayed, we decided to send them a bouquet of flowers with a note saying, "I am so sorry for your loss. I understand that something like this would be very emotional and upsetting. I do hope that one day you might realize that the neighborhood is an extremely desirable area and that you can still enjoy your home."

We didn't hear anything from them until eight months later. They called and said they had been to a church service and the pastor talked about love and forgiveness. They felt convicted, as they did not show anything like that toward me, yet I did toward them. They asked me if I would forgive them. I told them I had, eight months ago, and that I had no ill feelings whatsoever toward them. They proceeded to tell me that they love the neighborhood and had decided that they would like to purchase a larger home in the same tract. They asked if I would sell their one story and find them a two story. I told them I would. I placed it on the market, sold it, and found a two story just a few doors away. The relationship was restored, they got their new home, and I prospered through it. They also learned a valuable lesson and realized they had falsely accused me. If I would not have responded with love and forgiveness, I can say confidently that I wouldn't have received the call for me to help them find another home. I would not have had those sales.

> Great peace have they which love thy law: and nothing
> shall offend them.
>
> —Psalm 119:165

The Bible makes a very powerful statement in 1 Corinthians 13:8, "Love never fails" (NKJV). That is a remarkable verse, to say it "never fails." What in life can we say "never" about? There is always some percentage of chance that something could occur or not occur, right? But God's Word declares something so definite to say "never." That assurance is extremely comforting to know. If we respond with love, we will always have the victory. (See Matthew 5:46; Luke 6:28.)

This was an extreme case, and I still didn't understand their anger toward me. But even the extreme God can change your situation!

CHAPTER 6

TEN DOLLARS BUYS MORE THAN A HUNDRED

THERE WAS A time when I had gone through a year of no income. There was a very good reason why this happened, as I will explain ahead. But first I would like to share a few stories.

At this time when I went through this yearlong financial dry spell, I had exhausted all funds and had tapped out the credit cards to a tune of $175,000. Although I was never late on even one bill, I would just borrow more to pay all the bills. My credit score was in the mid 800s, and had always been, so I was able to borrow much. However, the day came when I was out of all money. My house payment of $1,800 was due on the first, and now it was twenty-nine days later and unpaid. On the thirtieth day they would file a thirty-day late on my credit, and I had never had a late notice. I very much valued my credit and didn't want a mark on it.

I was holding an open house on a Sunday, the twenty-ninth day past the due date of my house payment. I was praying and thanking God for the money to pay it by the next day, as that would be the last day before a late notice. I was reminding Him that I had always been a tither. In Isaiah 43:26 He said to put Him in remembrance of His Word (not that He forgets but to show Him we are trusting in Him), and His Word says to prove Him in Malachi 3:10, that He would provide. This is a promise to only those who tithe. I had been one, at that point, for twenty-four years. The Bible tells us to tithe to the church we attend and where we are a member.

Well, about an hour later, in walks a woman who said, "I am looking for Bill Wiese, and I recognize that you are he." She was conservatively dressed, soft-spoken, kind, and a very pleasant lady. She went on to say, "This morning I was thinking about you, how when you sold me my home five years ago you had to cut your commission in order for me to get the house." Now understand, it's the seller who pays the commission not the buyer, and she was the buyer. Why would she remember that fact and even think about it that Sunday? Well, she then handed me $2,000 in cash and said, "I just felt to give you this money. I don't know how much commission you gave up for me, but I just felt to give this to you today."

Well, that gave me 10 percent to tithe (Mal. 3:10; Matt. 23:23) and left $1,800 to make my house payment. I didn't receive a late notice, because I went right to the bank and paid the mortgage the next morning. The Lord came through at the last moment. Now I don't know how many people have handed you twenty one-hundred-dollar bills before on the very day you needed it, but I know that it was God telling her to do it. She was not a Christian, and I hadn't seen or heard from her in five years. The reason this happened is because God is a good God and wants to bless us, but we must be tithers for God to do that for us. It's not that we earn it, but He is the one who told us to tithe. (Mal. 3:8) and said, "Prove me now herewith, saith the LORD of hosts, if I will not open you the windows of heaven, and pour you out a blessing, that there shall not be room enough to receive it" (v. 10). God said to prove Him. It's like Him saying, "I dare you to trust Me with a tenth of what I have given you." There is no other place in Scripture where He says to prove Him. He is the one who gives us the money in the first place. I believe He says to prove Him here because in regard to money, most won't let go of it, and by paying our tithes, it breaks greed in our lives. It proves to Him that we trust Him, even with our "precious" money.

PS: I did claim that $2,000 on my tax return, as God cannot continue to bless us if we don't render unto Caesar and keep the laws of the land.

At the Last Minute

Another incident that occurred during this lean time financially was when I had written a check for $445 to pay a bill. I hadn't balanced the checkbook, and when I did, it was at zero, before writing the check. I had already mailed it, and I had never given a bad check before. I had no funds to cover the check and no more borrowing ability. I began praying, and about two hours later, I received a call from an escrow company. The woman asked for Bill Wiese, and I said, "It is I." She said that fifteen years ago there was an escrow that had closed and the check was never paid to me. It was lost in a file, and they just found it. Now understand, escrow law in California requires any funds not paid must be given to the state after seven years. However, the check was issued but lost. They must have had an overage in their trust account but somehow missed it for fifteen years. They said the check was for $556 and would I like them to mail it. I said, "No, I'll come pick it up right away!" It was a small amount, but it was enough to cover my bad check and pay my tithe. Tell me that isn't God! There is no chance that would ever happen, much less on the very day I needed it and almost to the dollar. Thank You, Lord, again.

> Cast thy bread upon the waters: for thou shalt find it
> after many days.
> —ECCLESIASTES 11:1

When you give to God, it will always come back to you, even if it takes a while (Prov. 19:17).

What Can Only Fifty Dollars Do?

One last story I will share, in regard to the lean time, even though there are many. It was during this time that I was out of money and also out of food. I had scraped up fifty dollars from a jar of change I had. I don't know if any of you have ever been there, but I'm sure some have. It's pretty bad when it gets to that point. I was hungry, but I decided to take the fifty dollars to our church and give it to the poor. Now I had no food and no money, but the Bible says to give to the poor and you will not lack, and it will be given back to you (Prov. 19:17; 22:9).

The next morning, I received a knock on my door. It was a neighbor from five doors down. I had never met him or his wife before. He said that they were leaving on an unexpected trip to Europe and had just gone shopping for food. They had bought all this food, healthy type foods, as they were health enthusiasts. Well, so am I, and I only eat healthy things such as good whole-grain bread, spring water, fresh fish, organic fruits and vegetables, free-range eggs; no dairy and no fast food; no burgers, fried food, soft drinks, and the like. The food they had purchased was all healthy, and they had said they had just spent five hundred dollars for it. That was ten times what I just gave the night before.

Again, I have never had someone whom I don't know knock on my door and offer me health food, especially on the very day I needed it. I'm telling you, this actually happened. Tell me tithing is not for today! Tell me it doesn't work! This same type of thing happened many times during that year of difficulty. Many other similar things also happened throughout my entire life. God has proven Himself over and over again.

> He that hath pity upon the poor lendeth unto the LORD; and that which he hath given will he pay him again.
>
> —PROVERBS 19:17

Unexpected Miracle

It was a Wednesday night, and I was at my brother and sister-in-law's home. I had always attended church on Wednesday nights, but this day my knee was in a lot of pain and I was feeling exhausted. It had not recovered from the surgery I had six months earlier. I had torn it up from doing squats at the gym. The surgery didn't take, and the doctor told me, "Some never do get better." I had never in my life had an injury, had never been sick, and had never even been to a doctor. I was always blessed with great health. Being athletic, it was so frustrating to not be able to do anything for six months. I was only about twenty-eight years old then. To go through surgery was a big deal to me. I was standing on the verse in Jeremiah 30:17, "For I will restore health unto thee, and I will heal thee of thy wounds, saith the LORD."

My sister-in-law wanted to make a nice dinner for me and was encouraging me to stay off my feet and just relax that evening. It sounded so tempting and would not have been any harm. But something inside was telling me to go to church. I couldn't shake it. So I declined my sister-in-law's tempting offer and dragged myself out the door for the forty-minute drive.

I came into the church and sat in the back row. I had just started going to this new church only a week prior and didn't know a soul. I was planning on paying my tithe that night of $2,500. However, during the service I felt prompted to give an additional $7,500 for an offering. I knew it was the Lord telling me to give it, because it wouldn't be my flesh. It also wouldn't be the devil, since he doesn't want the church having any money to help spread the gospel. It was a lot of money for me to give at that time, but I felt led to do it.

I wrote the check and placed it in the bucket. The pastor began preaching. About halfway through his message he abruptly stopped mid-sentence and said, "There is someone here who has a bad knee, and I am to pray for you." He then pointed to me and said, "It's you." How could he have known? (Only by the word of knowledge, a gift from the Lord.) There were approximately three hundred people in the service, and I was all the way in the back. No one even noticed me come in, and when I came in on the crutches, the pastor hadn't even arrived yet. So he didn't know I was on crutches, as they were lying on the floor.

He came off the stage all the way to the back to me and laid his hands on the injured knee, which he wouldn't have known which one it was as it wasn't taped. Nothing happened at that moment. However, the very next morning, I woke up and got out of bed carefully, as I had been doing, but my knee was completely healed! There was no pain, and I didn't need the crutches anymore. I had been in excruciating pain for six months, and now it was totally gone. Oh, thank You, God! That was a major miracle, and I was ecstatic.

Two points to mention: what if I would have stayed home at my brother and sister-in-law's, as I so wanted to do? What if I wouldn't have given the Lord's tithe and my offering?

Now, you can't buy a healing from God, but obedience is rewarded. Malachi 4:2 says, "But unto you who *fear* my name shall the Sun of Righteousness arise with *healing* in his wings" (emphasis added). And in Deuteronomy 14:22–23 it states, "Thou shalt truly *tithe* all the increase of thy seed...that thou mayest learn to *fear* the LORD thy God always" (emphasis added). One more verse is Job 36:11, which says, "If they obey and serve him, they shall spend their days in prosperity, and their years in pleasures."

Living with excruciating pain is not pleasurable! Obedience to God's Word brings blessings. The Bible says to tithe that you may learn to fear the Lord. In other words, if you don't tithe, you haven't learned the fear of the Lord. If you do fear Him by showing Him through the tithe, healing will arise in His wings for you. That is what happened for me. I know if I wouldn't have gone to church that night and wouldn't have given in the offering,

I wouldn't have been healed. This is not a works trip or legalism. It does not have to do with salvation or earning anything from God. However, the blessings of God are not automatic but only come through obedience to His Word. We serve a great God.

> He is a rewarder of them that diligently seek Him.
> —HEBREWS 11:6

> If ye be willing and obedient, ye shall eat the good of the land.
> —ISAIAH 1:19

> He that feareth the commandment shall be rewarded.
> —PROVERBS 13:13

> By the word of thy lips I have kept me from the paths of the destroyer.
> —PSALM 17:4

For further study, read: Exodus 15:26; 23:25; Psalm 41:3; Isaiah 53:5; Matthew 18:19; Acts 10:38; 1 Peter 2:24.

Why Did I Have a Year of No Income?

You say, "I thought tithing would always cause you to prosper, Bill? So why did you go through such a shortage?" There is more in the Word of God than only tithing. We must obey in other areas as well. Ahead I list some of the things we must do in order to live a prosperous life. And they are a combination of all the Word working together.

Here is the reason I had this dry year of no income: There was something I had done that God told me not to do. He told me clearly not to become a board member of a church I was attending. I didn't hear an audible voice, but I did hear that inner voice, a strong sense of knowing. You simply have this "knowing" inside, when it's from God.

Now there was nothing wrong with being a board member, but He didn't want me to be one. Well, the pastor and leaders of the church felt that I should based on my real estate background, my friendship with the pastor, and my lifestyle. They meant well, but they were just looking at outside circumstances. On the surface, that seemed a good thing. But for other reasons, God didn't want me involved, especially with the church finances. I kept telling them no, but they persisted. Finally, one day, I conceded. I said to myself, "Well, I guess I missed God, and they all must be right." I accepted and was now the treasurer on the board.

Wrong decision! I had trusted their opinion over what I strongly believed God had told me, which was no. I officially became a board member on July 9 of that year. Well, that was the last day I made any money, until the following July 9, the next year. One whole year I worked very hard and didn't make a penny. It was the following July 9 that I had made a sale, on that exact date. At this time in my life, I was making approximately $250,000 per year. And now, zero for the year. You say, "Why, Bill, would God be so severe and strict?" I can tell you why. It was because I was a mature Christian and knew better. I had heard His voice a thousand times in the past, and why would I doubt it now, and why take the word of another over God's word?

There are many examples of even greater severity in the Bible, but just to give you one. In 1 Kings 13, there was a young prophet who was told that when he went to Bethel, he was not to eat with anyone, and when he left, to go another way. Then on the way out of the town, he came across an old prophet who asked him to come and eat with him. He first said no, he couldn't, as he was told by God. The old prophet said that an angel told him it would be all right. So the young prophet believed him and went to his house and ate. Then when he left the house, on his way, a lion slew him and he died.

You say, "That is so severe." Yes, but God told him and he listened to another instead. The old prophet had lied to him. No angel had really told him that it was all right to eat. Even if an angel had told him, it would have been a lying devil, since God told the young prophet no. So he lost his life. I lost a year's income, not nearly as bad as losing your life. Now I am not comparing myself with a prophet in any way, but my point is that God's Word is the same for us all to obey. God never changes. I am glad God wasn't as strict with me as He was with the prophet.

I do understand that we are under grace and are not to be legalistic. I also understand that God would be stricter with one of His prophets than with the everyday person. And I am again not to be compared to a prophet. The point is, God was attempting to teach me that I should have trusted His voice after all these years. However, God still took care of me as I was able to never be late on even one bill, I had a roof over my head, and I was fed. He maintained my life even through all of that. God is faithful, but He expects obedience.

Isn't Tithing "Under the Law"?

If there is one thing I have found in the Bible that is one of the most important keys to success and pleasing to God, it is tithing. A tithe means a tenth (Gen. 14:20; Heb. 7:2–4). Since I first discovered this principle and command of God, my life has never had lack, and every bill has always been paid on time. This has been true for forty-one years as a Christian. During all the years

I had been in the real estate business, I had never had a paycheck coming in each week, as my income was commission based. Yet, I never missed a payment. In addition, through all the difficult and poor economic periods, I have never had even one late notice. Every bill has been paid on time. That is truly a testimony of God's faithfulness. His Word never fails.

Of course, there are many things in God's Word for us to obey, but this is one of the main keys for success. We are to tithe to the church we attend. You say, "But tithing is only in the Old Testament, and today we should give by our heart." No, tithing is also in the New Testament and also prior to the Law. And yes, we are to give out of a heart's desire to please God, but many believe their heart is telling them to give less than 10 percent. That is the reason they are saying, "It is in the Old Testament." They are trying to find a way out of giving the tenth. Yet, we should be actually giving more than just 10 percent, as we now have an even better covenant (Heb. 8:6).

First of all, Jesus mentioned tithing and said you should not omit it (Matt. 23:23; Luke 11:42). Hebrews 7:2–4 points out how Abraham gave a tenth of all. (See Genesis 14:20.)

Jesus also said in Matthew 5:17, "Think not that I am come to destroy the law…but to fulfil." As far as it being "under the law," it was also prior to the Law. Abraham was four hundred years before the Law was given, and he tithed. Cain and Able also tithed (Gen. 4:3–4). That was, of course, prior to the Law. There are many other verses in regard to tithing, as I have listed here: Genesis 14:20; 28:22; Leviticus 27:32; Numbers 18:26; Deuteronomy 12:6, 14:22–23; 26:12; 2 Chronicles 31:5–6, 12; Nehemiah 10:38; 13:12; Proverbs 3:9–10; Ezekiel 45:14; Malachi 3:8–11.

In Deuteronomy 14:23 it states we are to tithe that we might learn the fear of the Lord. In other words, if we don't tithe, we don't fear the Lord. God said it, not me. If you argue, then obviously you haven't learned to respect *all* of the Word. Also it says in Deuteronomy 17:19, "He shall read therein all the days of his life: that he may learn to *fear* the LORD his God, to keep all the words of this law and these statutes, to do them" (emphasis added).

You would need to eliminate all those verses above to say tithing is not for today. The question you would have to ask yourself is, "Why am I looking for a way out?"

It takes money to promote the gospel. It takes money to give away Bibles, books, tapes, and to travel and preach. It takes big money to go on television and radio. Where do you think the money comes from to pay for all of this? Some people will say, "Well, I don't care about having abundance. I just need to pay my bills, and that is enough." That is being very selfish, if all you care about is yourself. The reason for tithing is so that we can be a blessing to others, help spread God's Word, and enjoy our life also. As long as the "things" don't have us, God wants us to prosper. Jesus said to "seek ye first the kingdom of God, and his righteousness; and all these things shall be added unto you" (Matt. 6:33).

There are some who tithe but have not had abundance in their lives. However, there are many reasons where we can miss God's Word. Just to mention a few things: honoring your parents that it might go well with you, operating in faith, showing love and forgiveness, repenting, being teachable, praying and reading His Word, walking in holiness, and so on. There is one verse that states, "Ye have sown much, and bring in little...he that earneth wages...put it into a bag with holes" (Hag. 1:6). God said, "Because of mine house that is waste...therefore the heaven over you is stayed from dew..." (vv. 9–10). God pointed out that they had homes for themselves but let God's house lay in waste. He said for them to "consider your ways" (v. 5). If we are not involved in building God's house, and His house is "souls" as well as the actual church building, and if we are not concerned about the salvation of others, we will not experience the blessings that come from tithing. If we do not tithe in the first place, we are under a curse (Mal. 3:8–9).

Why would anyone want to find a way out of tithing? Our attitude should be a joyful one in our giving and looking for ways to give even more than 10 percent. If you give out of only trying to avoid the curse, your heart is wrong, and God loves a cheerful giver (2 Cor. 9:7). God also instructs us to give offerings, which are above the amount of the tithe.

In my career I had sold over one thousand homes and did not have one complaint, lawsuit, or serious problem whatsoever. This is not to brag on myself but on God. This would be impossible without God. One of the promises to the tither is that God will rebuke the devourer for our sake (Mal. 3:11). I'm simply pointing out that He did that for me for thirty-five years in the business alone. Of course, I was very careful and diligent in my work. I always had everything put in writing, with no compromises of legality or of ethics. I checked out every detail myself in regard to the property and so forth. However, even with those good work habits, I would not have had a perfect record, by far, without God. He has been so gracious to me. Because we tithe, we don't have things stolen from us or break down. He preserves and lengthens the use of our material things, just as the Israelites had when wandering in the desert for forty years and their shoes didn't wear out (Deut. 29:5). That's what He has done for us.

If you want to say that tithing is only for the Old Testament and claim you only live in the New, then look at Acts 2:44–45. They had sold all things and divided them among all men, and had all things in common. In other words, they gave *all* and not just 10 percent.

In addition, I can give you some examples where Jesus raised the bar in the New Testament, so tithes should follow suit.

In the Old Testament, it was a sin if one committed adultery. But in the New Testament, if you look with lust, it is the same as committing adultery (Matt. 5:27–28). If you murdered someone in the Old Testament, you were in danger of the judgment. But in the New Testament, if you are angry without a cause, you are in danger of the judgment (Matt. 5:21–22). In the Old Testament, if you killed someone, you were considered a murderer. But in the New Testament, if you even hate your brother without a cause, you are considered a murderer (1 John 3:15). In the New Testament, if you only call someone a fool, you are in danger of hell fire (Matt. 5:22). My point is, if you are going to throw out the Old Testament and say you only live in the New, then the standard is now much higher, and you should tithe even more than 10 percent.

Phil Pringle says, "The tithe has never belonged to us. The first tenth of our income is always God's. As mature Christians, it should be unthinkable to hold our hand out for a blessing from God, when we have His property in our other hand."[1]

If you want to struggle, experience lack, and have things stolen, then continue not to tithe. We cannot pick and choose the parts out of the Word that we think are correct. We must obey all of it. Do you think God would be pleased with your editing?

Twenty Percent Interest Charged?

When I first got into the real estate business, I worked for three years and earned approximately six thousand dollars per year. This was below average, but it was more than it sounds today. The years were from 1973–1976. After three years of this mediocre income and no increase, a Christian woman asked me, "Do you tithe?" I told her that I had never heard of it. I hadn't studied the Bible very much those first three years. She told me that if I tithed and gave offerings, as the Bible tells us to do, I would prosper much more. Well, I read all the verses I could find and discovered that I was missing an important command of God and an important promise of prosperity. I also found a verse that states, "If a man will at all redeem ought of his tithes, he shall add thereto the fifth part thereof" (Lev. 27:31).

In other words, if we don't pay our tithes, we owe an additional 20 percent. So I not only owed three years of back tithes, but 20 percent on top of it. I then figured out how much I owed and decided to pay it back. I decided to pay 20 percent tithe until I was caught up.

Now, some might think that sounds like legalism, but I simply saw it as obedience to the Word. I wanted to do everything I could find in the Bible. I wanted all God had for me. The first year I began tithing the 10 percent. I thought that I would start paying back the 20 percent on the second year. After the first year, my income went from $6,000 to $12,000. Then I began paying the tithe plus the 20 percent amount, and my income went from $12,000 to $18,000. Then the next year went to $40,000, then $80,000, then $160,000. It continued to increase every year. God has always prospered us, and the 20 percent is part of His Word.

You can say I'm into legalism, but I have found that every word in the Bible is true and for us today. You can't pick and choose. It all works.

After years of tithing, I learned in Deuteronomy 26 that we are to tithe the tithe. In other words, we don't just drop our tithe in the bucket as it passes. There is a time we are to spend in prayer, and a certain prayer that it spells out that we should be praying. It states just how to pray and what our attitude should be. It is taking the time to thank God for what He has done. This is not to be ignored just because it is Old Testament. It clearly shows us the thankful attitude we are to maintain. My wife and I have done this, and we have experienced the good measure, pressed down, and running over. We chose to obey His Word in all areas. To us, each of these things found in His Word is a treasure (Prov. 2:1–6).

CHAPTER 7

MORE HONESTY, LESS FLATTERY

I HAD THIS PROPERTY that wouldn't seem to sell. The owner was an old, bitter man, and no matter how hard I worked, he always complained and found fault. One day he called, screaming and yelling, making all these unreasonable demands and griping about every little thing. He called constantly, complaining, and became extremely irritating. This continued for several weeks. I finally said to him, "You can keep your listing. I don't want it any longer. I have done all I can do and much more than what is required. I don't want to work with someone as negative and bitter as you, so I'm canceling the listing."

Now in the beginning, this man flattered me all the time.

He was always telling me and everyone around him how great I was. I didn't like him doing that, and in addition, I knew it wasn't genuine. Even if it was real, I wouldn't have liked it. If something nice is said about you once or twice, that's all right. But when it's constant, you know something is wrong. I asked myself the question, "Why are you working with this guy? He will most likely be difficult." However, I just went on with it and figured it wouldn't be too long.

Later that evening, after I had told him I was canceling the listing, he called back and said, "I'm sorry. You were right. I have been bitter, negative, and faultfinding, and I didn't realize how difficult I have been. Would you please consider continuing to be my agent?" I told him, "All right, I will continue."

Proverbs 28:23 says, "He that rebuketh a man afterwards shall find more favour than he that flattereth with the tongue."

He was an intimidating man, and sometimes we don't like to stand up to those types of individuals. Doing what Scripture instructs us to do resulted in a sale. I ended up selling the home a week later.

In addition to learning that rebuking someone at the right time can be scriptural, notice also how flattery is dangerous. Look at these verses:

> He that speaketh flattery to his friends, even the eyes of his children shall fail.
>
> —JOB 17:5

> Their throat is an open sepulchre; they flatter with their tongue [the wicked]. Destroy thou them, O God; let them fall by their own counsels.
>
> —PSALM 5:9–10

For he flattereth himself in his own eyes, until his iniquity be found to be hateful.

—PSALM 36:2

In other words, if it continues, it gets worse and grows to hate.

To deliver thee from the strange woman, even from the stranger which flattereth with her words....For her house inclineth unto death, and her paths unto the dead.

—PROVERBS 2:16–18

Meddle not with him that flattereth with his lips.

—PROVERBS 20:19

A man that flattereth his neighbour spreadeth a net for his feet.

—PROVERBS 29:5

And such as do wickedly against the covenant shall he corrupt by flatteries...yet they shall fall by the sword, and by flame, by captivity...

—DANIEL 11:32

All the things God instructs us to do are for our own benefit. The things He says to avoid are truly detrimental to us.

CHAPTER 8

DETERMINED, NOT DESPERATE

THERE WAS A time when the real estate market was doing well for the first half of the year. Thankfully, I too had a very good first half. I had paid my quarterly estimates for income tax, which are based on the preceding year's income. However, I had made substantially more money for those first six months. Yet, the second half of the year I did not do as well and had not saved much. I was young and not doing some of the more prudent things at that time. Well, next year it came time to prepare our tax return, and I discovered I owed an additional $45,000 over and above my quarterly estimates that had been paid. I didn't have the money, and it was due April 15, which was in two and a half weeks!

I knew I needed to pray and fast, and God would give me

the answer. I decided on a three-day fast. I had also learned from Isaiah 58:6–11 to take clothes and food down to the mission for the poor. I went out and purchased the food and clothes and took them down the first day.

On the second day of the fast, I received a call from a past client who simply called to say hello. We had become friends during the many past transactions. He mentioned that he had been looking for a home on the ocean during the past six months. I said, "Why didn't you tell me so I could find you one?"

He said, "Bill, to get a good oceanfront home you really need to specialize in that area and have an inroad. You don't work that area, so you wouldn't get the inside scoop." And he was right.

However, I said, "Let me go and see what I can find."

He said that he had looked at everything on the market for the last six months with some of the top specialists in the area and had not found what he was looking for. "So, Bill, you can't show me something I haven't already seen."

I replied, "Well, if I find something you haven't seen, will you go and take a look?"

He said, "Sure I will."

I checked the computer and then went down to the beach to begin searching.

Everything I had found, he had already seen. On the second day of my search, which was the third day of my fast, I had come across a home that was a famous historic landmark in the city. I thought it was a home he would like, if he hadn't already seen it. I called him and asked him. It was the old Bette Davis estate. He said, "No, no one has bothered to show me that one," as it is a famous landmark property and most didn't even consider it. I don't know why not.

We drove to the house, walked in the front door, and he immediately liked it and said, "This is it! It needs a lot of remodeling, but the bones are good." And it was.

He then said, "Bill, I need to be able to close escrow within two weeks. I'll pay cash. Can you do it?"

I said, "No problem. I think we can handle that!" So we did, and it closed two days prior to my due date of April 15. My commission check was $54,000, which gave me enough to tithe and pay the tax bill. Thank God!

Now, I don't think anyone could say it was a coincidence. I had never received a check that large. The fact that he would have called me the first day of my fast, that I would find him a home he hadn't already seen with all the experts, and that his desire was to close in two weeks? No, there is not a chance. God did that. And if I was not a tither, it wouldn't have happened. Even with praying, I could not pray in faith that God would move on my behalf if I was not obeying His Word. He said to tithe, or we would be under a curse (Mal. 3:8–9). How can you rob God and then expect Him to help you financially? You might think you're not robbing Him, but I have found out that His Word, all of His Word, is "the same yesterday, today and forever" (Heb. 13:8).

Now in addition, I also had to press in with the prayer and fasting. I had to be persistent with my client and get to work. Sitting around wouldn't have gotten the results. It is a combination of applying the principles in God's Word and going out and doing it. God will then make it happen. If we obey, we will be blessed.

Isaiah 58:6–9 says, "Is not this the fast that I have chosen?... Is it not to deal thy bread to the hungry?... Then shalt thou call, and the LORD shall answer; thou shalt cry, and he shall say, Here I am." How's that for a promise!

Not a Chance!

I had listed a property and found out it had a cracked foundation. The crack was underneath the carpeting, so it was not obvious at first. After further investigation, by obtaining an engineering report, I discovered it was a major crack and the house was sliding toward the slope in the rear. After a long time, we found a buyer who felt he could repair it since he was in the construction business. During the escrow, the buyer ended up being rejected by seven different lenders along with the property due to its condition. In addition, after he had fully investigated the property, he decided the problem to repair it was too costly. He canceled the escrow.

I was newly married and was really counting on the money from this sale. Two weeks had passed after the cancellation, so it was long dead. Well, my wife said, "No, we are not giving up. This buyer is coming back, and he will qualify and desire to purchase this home." Well, I had zero faith in her statement, as the transaction had been dead for two weeks. Besides, the buyer tried seven different lenders and couldn't get a loan, and the property was cracked in half and slipping down a hillside.

Annette didn't look at all that, but only considered that we had a covenant with God. The Word says that everything we set our hand to do shall prosper, and God commands a blessing on all that we undertake (Deut. 28). Galatians 3:29 says we are heirs of Abraham and blessed according to the promise. We know Abraham was blessed financially. So, for a week, my wife spoke out of her own mouth many verses in regard to God's provision.

After that week, we received a call from the buyer. He said that in the last few days he couldn't stop thinking about that house and felt he should try one more time with a credit union to qualify to obtain the loan. He said he couldn't get it out of his mind and thought he could repair it. I was shocked, to say the least. A week later, the credit union approved him and the property, and the sale closed.

That was definitely God, but it wouldn't have occurred if my wife hadn't exercised faith and stood on God's promises. Sometimes we have to get aggressive and even angry when something is being stolen from us by the enemy. Matthew 11:12 says, "The kingdom of heaven suffereth violence, and the violent take it by force." First Peter 5:8 says, "The devil walks about like a roaring lion, seeking whom he may devour" (NKJV). John 10:10 says, "The thief [Satan] does not come except to steal, and to kill and to destroy" (NKJV).

It was not my faith, but my wife's that caused that sale to happen (Matt. 9:22; Mark 5:34; 10:52; Luke 8:48; 17:19). Of course, it is God who does it all, and it is by His grace. However, He is moved by our faith in Him (James 1:6–7). God delights to perform His Word, and faith is what pleases Him (Heb. 11:6). I thank the Lord again and my wonderful wife. I married way over my head!

Diligence

Another time, a large construction company had called me. I was referred to them by a woman I knew. They were looking for a company to sell off eighteen condominiums that were remaining in a new project they had built. It was during the time of the early nineties down market. I was, again, up against the larger real estate companies, just as in a prior situation. I explained to the owner of the company that I didn't have the manpower or the advertising budget that the larger companies had, but I did know more about the project than anyone else.

I had done all my homework for three months before meeting

with her, plus I had been working in the field for years in that area. I had a spreadsheet of twenty-five different new complexes that were being built at that time, and I had looked at each one. I had gathered all the facts and information. I knew the marketplace and had sold condos for a builder before. I had thoroughly done all the research on financing and so forth.

I was prepared. I proceeded to show her that her prices were too high to compete with so many others in a soft market. I showed her what the prices should be and gave her a projected time frame of the completion. I had much paperwork prepared to back my opinion. I made it a point to know more than any of my competition. She then said, "You have obviously done a lot of research, and I can see all the facts you have gathered. I would rather have someone who has knowledge than someone who has money or manpower. We will provide the advertising; you just handle the prospects. I like your honesty, and I like that you have put a great deal of effort and time into something that you didn't know you would get. If you will work this hard on an unknown, then how much more so on something known. You got the job."

I have learned to work diligently and put every effort into something in every situation. I ended up selling all eighteen units and, again, received a glowing letter of commendation.

> Seest thou a man diligent in his business? he shall stand before kings; he shall not stand before mean men.
> —PROVERBS 22:29

> The heart of the righteous studieth to answer.
> —PROVERBS 15:28

CHAPTER 9

COMMITTED, NOT COMPROMISED

I RECEIVED A CALL from a man who owned one of the largest commercial construction companies in California. He wanted to interview me to list his home. Being in the construction industry, he knew many real estate agents, many being heavy hitters. I was from a small company, which was my own.

During the interview he brought up the subject of religion, as he had heard I was a Christian. By his own words, he was not. He was very strong in his views and was opposed to the biblical view. For some reason, he wanted to debate each issue. I said to him, "I strongly disagree with your view, and I can refute each point you bring up if you would like to hear it." He said, "Yes, I would." So I did and gave him correct information to help him see his misconceptions.

By the end of our discussion, I figured he was not going to employ me, but it didn't really matter. I cared more about giving him clear and straight answers regarding the Bible than I did about listing his property. To my surprise, he finally commented, "You got the job." He went on to say, "You stood your ground and didn't back off, made good convincing arguments, and were not concerned if you pleased me or not to get the listing. I like that strength. If you were that strong with me, then you will be strong in convincing a prospective buyer toward my house."

He saw that I would not quit or be timid. Even though he disagreed intensely on religion, he didn't let that stand in the way. My concern for him to obtain the truth impressed him more than my concern for the listing. The moral is, put God first and He will provide (Matt. 6:33).

Expressing Genuine Care

As a side note, I didn't have an argumentative or condescending attitude, but only a committed and concerned one. I would never force my beliefs on anyone. Strength is admired if accompanied by an honest concern for others. I believe if our motive is to express a genuine care, then even a disagreeable position can be more easily swallowed. The wisdom from God is needed in order to know how to act and react with all different types of people.

> The king's favour is toward a wise servant.
> —PROVERBS 14:35

By the way, I did list and sell the property in a very short time, and we got along nicely.

CHAPTER 10

THE ONLY GUARANTEE
AGAINST FAILURE

T HERE WAS A certain elderly woman who would call me every week for a period of seven years. She would ask me to help her with whatever problems she had in her home, such as plumbing, appliances needing repair, and so forth. She resided in the neighborhood in which I lived and worked. Once a week I would stop by and help her. She was a licensed real estate agent and worked for a competing office in the neighborhood I sold homes in. I think she was just lonely, as her husband had died several years earlier. One day she called me and said she wanted me to list her home for sale. I asked, "Why would you list it with me when you are in the business?" She replied, "Because you have done so much for me these seven years. I believe you would be a hard worker and do a better job than myself."

I went over to her home and listed the house. During that time, she asked me why I never pushed my "religion," as she called it, on her. She knew I was a Christian, and she was completely opposed to it. I explained to her that I understood she was against the Bible and that I would never push my beliefs on anyone, that God is a gentleman. You see, if someone is interested in God, then they need to ask about Him themselves sometimes. We have to be sensitive and know when to share with them and when to refrain. Well, my silence spoke volumes, and my consistent display of love left her hungry to know more. I then shared with her God's plan of salvation. She ended up accepting the Lord Jesus as her Lord and Savior. I sold her home and it ended well. The Bible says, "Love never fails" (1 Cor. 13:8, NKJV). Our actions do speak louder than words.

One Vote Makes the Difference

I was sitting at an open house, and a nice older couple came in. They were so pleasant, kind, and well dressed. They wanted to lease a home rather than purchase the one I had for sale. So I told them about a home I had seen in the neighborhood that had a "For Lease by Owner" sign in the window. We decided to walk over together to find out more information. When we got to the house, I knocked on the door and asked the owner if she was still looking to lease her home. She immediately screamed at me and told me how she hated real estate agents and would never work with one. I said, "I understand, and I know some agents can be difficult, but you can just work with this couple directly. I don't need to be involved in any way. I don't want any money. They really need a place, and I am sure they would be just what you are looking for."

Well, she slammed the door in my face. I asked the nice couple to go back to her later and see if she would talk to them without me there. They did, and she leased it to them. After I learned that everything had worked out very well, I sent a thank-you note and a flower arrangement to the owner who slammed the door, saying, "Thank you for taking care of them."

Years rolled by, and I would occasionally run into the nice couple. Six years went by, and at this time I was the president of the homeowners association in this same neighborhood. The entire complex needed to be painted. It was a PUD, or Planned Unit Development, and they were called "patio homes." All the units were the same 1970s beige color. We were proposing to have it changed from the one color to a variety of coordinated color schemes. We were hiring one of the top companies in America to do the color scheme. The addition of colors would add a cost to each homeowner of four hundred dollars. This was a two-year battle to get the people to even consider changing the color scheme. It sometimes is difficult to institute change in people's lives, even if it is an improvement.

We needed a majority vote. It came to the final night for the vote, and at this point we were only one vote short of passing. At the meeting, one of the homeowners stood up and asked to speak. This was the woman who had slammed the door in my face and hated real estate people. She said, "I'm going to vote for the painting and go along with Bill Wiese's recommendation to change the colors. He looked out for a nice elderly couple once, and also for me, so I'm sure he is looking out for us now. So he has my vote." With that said, we had our ninety-three votes, and the motion passed by one.

This story shows that if we demonstrate the love of God toward people, even when they treat us poorly, it will always come back to bless us later. Jesus said in Matthew 5:44–46, "Love your enemies, bless those who curse you, do good to those who hate you" (NKJV). "But if you love those who love you, what credit is that to you? For even sinners love those who love them" (Luke 6:32, NKJV).

In other words, showing love to those you love does not deserve a commendation. The test is to show love to those who "despitefully use you, and persecute you" (Matt. 5:44). Again, love never fails. Who would have known that my looking out for that homeowner would result in her trust in me six years later? By the way, most all of the people in the neighborhood ended up loving all the color changes.

CHAPTER 11

A PILOT'S CHECKLIST

BEFORE A PILOT takes off on his flight, he has a checklist of things to observe to be certain all is in good working order. If he forgets to check it, he may miss something, and that could cost him his life. This awareness causes him to be extremely careful not to make any mistakes. Well, as Christians, we should be as diligent in our everyday lives. Our desire should be to search the Scriptures to see if we are missing something God's Word instructs us to do. I know we are under grace, but I am not talking about earning anything from God or obeying by our own power. It is His grace that enables us to obey His Word. Hebrews 12:28 states, "Let us have grace, whereby we may serve God acceptably with reverence and godly fear." In order to grow from glory to glory, we need to place more of His Word in our hearts. Psalm 119:11 states, "Thy word have I hid in mine heart, that I might not sin against thee."

When something goes wrong in our life, my wife and I first examine ourselves in light of the Word of God. Usually it is because I missed it somewhere. This is not a condemning remark, but instead, a welcomed heed to correction. We want to be sure that what we are doing lines up with Scripture. The Bible says to judge ourselves and not others (Matt. 7:1; 1 Cor. 11:31). If we can be honest, it takes humility to receive instruction and to admit we may have missed it.

> *Teach* me good judgment and knowledge.
> —PSALM 119:66, EMPHASIS ADDED

> Give me understanding, that I may *learn* thy commandments.
> —PSALM 119:73, EMPHASIS ADDED

> A wise man will hear, and will increase *learning.*
> —PROVERBS 1:5, EMPHASIS ADDED

> For the commandment is a lamp, and the law is light; and reproofs of instruction are the way of life.
> —PROVERBS 6:23

> He is in the way of life that keepeth instruction.
> —PROVERBS 10:17

> Whoso loveth instruction loveth knowledge.
> —PROVERBS 12:1

> But he that regardeth reproof shall be honoured.
> —PROVERBS 13:18

> Apply thine heart unto instruction.
> —PROVERBS 23:12

Study to shew thyself approved unto God.

—2 TIMOTHY 2:15, EMPHASIS ADDED

All scripture is given by inspiration of God, and is profitable for doctrine, for reproof, for correction, for instruction in righteousness.

—2 TIMOTHY 3:16

Here are some additional verses about instruction: Proverbs 1:2–3, 7–8; 4:13; 8:33; 13:1, 18; 19:20; Jeremiah 35:13; Zephaniah 3:7.

For God to prosper us, there are certain requirements He has spelled out in His Word.

1. Seek Him.

In Matthew 6:33, Jesus said, "But seek ye first the kingdom of God, and his righteousness; and all these things shall be added unto you." All what things? All the things He mentioned in the previous verses, such as treasures upon earth or what you shall eat, or drink, or wear. We are not to seek these things first. We are to seek the kingdom first.

What does it mean to seek the kingdom? When Jesus prayed for people to be healed, He said, "The kingdom of God has come nigh unto you" (Luke 10:9). Part of His kingdom is healing. He also said to pray, "Thy kingdom come. Thy will be done" (Matt. 6:9–10). Part of the kingdom is His will being done on the earth. His will is what He did on the earth, such as healing all (Acts 10:38), casting out devils (Mark 16:15–18), and preaching repentance (Matt. 4:17). He went about teaching and preaching the gospel (Matt. 4:23) and told us to preach the gospel, which is the news of salvation, of setting people free from bondages, laying hands on the sick, and feeding the poor (Isa. 61:1–2; Matt. 25:35–36; Mark 16:15). He said He would make us fishers of men (Matt. 4:19). In addition, it says in 2 Corinthians 8:9,

"That though he was rich, yet for your sakes he became poor, that ye through his poverty might be rich." Jesus also said in Luke 4:18, "The Spirit of the Lord is upon me because he hath anointed me to preach the gospel to the poor." Part of His kingdom is to prosper us (Deut. 8:18; 28:2). How could we feed the poor and support the gospel if we are broke ourselves? Colossians 3:2 states, "Set your affection on things above, not on things on the earth." So let us understand that He will not prosper us unless we are committed to seeking Him first.

2. Help the poor.

> Blessed is he that considereth the poor: the LORD will deliver him in time of trouble.
>
> —PSALM 41:1

> He hath dispersed, he hath given to the poor; his righteousness endureth for ever.
>
> —PSALM 112:9

> He that hath pity upon the poor lendeth unto the Lord; and that which he hath given will he pay him again.
>
> —PROVERBS 19:17

> The righteous giveth and spareth not.
>
> —PROVERBS 21:26

> He that hath a bountiful eye shall be blessed; for he giveth of his bread to the poor.
>
> —PROVERBS 22:9

> He that giveth unto the poor shall not lack: but he that hideth his eyes shall have many a curse.
>
> —PROVERBS 28:27

> Give, and it shall be given unto you; good measure, pressed down, and shaken together, and running over, shall men give into your bosom.
>
> —LUKE 6:38

All throughout the Bible it instructs us to help the poor. Jesus gave the story of the Good Samaritan (Luke 10:33) and others. It is the giving of ourselves for the welfare of others.

Tommy Barnett said, "The secret to a successful, happy life is giving yourself away. According to the Bible, you will succeed in direct proportion to how much you give yourself away.... Giving is truly the key to blessing... because we have learned to focus more and more on servanthood, downward mobility, on giving everything away."

He goes on to say, "We are conditioned to think in terms of limits, and therefore the world operates on the principle of lack.... God approaches life from the opposite angle. He operates on the principle of plenty. In God's kingdom, the successful man or woman is the one who gives the most away. The world says, 'He who dies with the most toys wins.' The kingdom says, 'He who gives the most away wins.' God doesn't see the cup as half full or half empty—He sees it overflowing!"[1]

Jesus also said in Matthew 6:19–21, "Do not lay up for yourselves treasures on earth, where moth and rust destroy and where thieves break in and steal; but lay up for yourselves treasures in heaven, where neither moth nor rust destroys and where thieves do not break in and steal. For where your treasure is, there your heart will be also" (NKJV). This is the only 100 percent safe investment. One way to lay up treasure in heaven is to, again, give to the poor (Matt. 19:21). Another is to teach the commandments (Matt. 5:19). For us to be about the Father's business is laying up treasures in heaven. My wife and I take every opportunity to give to God's kingdom, above the tithe. It is not only finances but also time, talent, and resources we are to give. We are investing in our eternity. In addition, God will bless us here on the earth if we do this (Mark 10:29–30).

3. Examine ourselves.

I mentioned earlier that when my wife and I are faced with life challenges, we take time out to pray, read God's Word, and examine ourselves to see where we may have missed the mark. This is a biblical exercise.

> Examine me, O LORD, and prove me; try my reins and my heart.
>
> —PSALM 26:2

> In the day of prosperity be joyful, but in the day of adversity *consider*: God also hath set the one over against the other.
>
> —ECCLESIASTES 7:14, EMPHASIS ADDED

> Let *us search* and try our ways.
>
> —LAMENTATIONS 3:40, EMPHASIS ADDED

> Thus saith the LORD of hosts; *Consider* your ways.
>
> —HAGGAI 1:7, EMPHASIS ADDED

> But *let a man* examine himself.
>
> —1 CORINTHIANS 11:28, EMPHASIS ADDED

> Examine yourselves, whether ye be in the faith; prove your own selves.
>
> —2 CORINTHIANS 13:5

4. Obey His Word.

I want to make it clear again that I am not talking about legalism. We are not trying to earn God's grace or to be burdened under "performance." We can't earn anything, as it has already been given to us freely. We are justified by Christ's blood and by faith in what He did for us on the cross only. (See Romans 3:24–25; 4:25; 5:9, 16, 18; Galatians 2:16; Ephesians 1:7; Colossians 1:14; Titus 3:7; 1 John 1:7–9.)

God's grace empowers us to obey His Word. (See Hebrews 12:28.) We cannot obey by our own power or ability but by His Spirit. The difference is, when you are truly in love with God, you are eager to please Him. It is not a burden to keep His Word but a delight. We keep His Word because of a heartfelt desire and not our performance (Ps. 119:16, 24, 47, 72).

David said in Psalm 119:16, "I will delight myself in thy statutes." When we understand His grace, there is a joy that comes to us, because we see it is not based on our power to keep His Word or resist sin, but by His power. However, searching the Scriptures to be sure we are obeying His Word doesn't nullify grace; being obedient to His Word is a result of grace. We are to continually strive to better ourselves by receiving correction from His Word. Our desire should be to grow from glory to glory. Our goal is to become more like Him (2 Cor. 3:18). If we say we love Him and do not obey Him, we are liars. We don't really love Him (1 John 2:3–4), and we don't know Him. Jesus said, "'If you love Me, keep My commandments'" (John 14:15, NKJV). Psalm 97:10 says, "You who love the LORD, hate evil!" (NKJV).

John Bevere said, "If you love God, you will have no trouble keeping His commandments! If serving God is an obligation, you have entered into a legalistic relationship, and it will be hard to keep His commandments. We should not serve God to earn His approval; we should serve God because we are in love with Him."[2]

In Psalm 119:32, David said, "I will run the way of thy commandments, when thou shalt enlarge my heart." In other words, as our heart is aroused toward God by our meditating in His Word, we will not have to force ourselves, in a sense, to obey His Word, but we will run for it in excitement. Verse 47 says, "And I will delight myself…" In verse 60 he said, "I made haste, and delayed not to keep thy commandments."

It is our attitude that makes the difference. An obedient heart seeks to please Him. In examining ourselves, we are not to feel that we cannot come to Him if we have not kept all these Scripture verses. No, because it is by grace that we receive the things we desire from Him. We do not try in our flesh to live holy. We live holy because we desire to, and it's by His grace we can do it.

However, some use grace as if it were a blanket to cover up their sin. And grace does cover, but not in the manner we have been taught. Grace does not alleviate our sin, but rather is an empowerment not to sin.

John Bevere states, "This lack of balance infiltrates our reasoning until we feel at complete liberty to disobey God whenever it is inconvenient or not to our advantage. Even as we sin we assure ourselves and quiet our consciences with a shrug and the thought, *God's grace will cover this, for He loves me and understands how tough life can be. He wants me happy, no matter the costs! Right?*.…Although grace covers, it is not merely a cover-up. It goes far beyond that. Grace enables and empowers us to live a life of holiness and obedience to the authority of God."[3]

John also states, "We've got the power of God's grace so we can set our sights on a life like Christ ('also to walk just as He walked'), for we are free from the control of the nature of disobedience."[4]

In addition, God loves us regardless of how we perform. We don't score points with God, and if we are good enough He will love us more. No, He loves us already the way we are. However, His desire is for us to grow and mature in Him. Anytime God corrects us, it is because He loves us. Hebrews 12:6 states, "Whom the LORD loves He chastens" (NKJV).

Andrew Wommack states, "Since God's love toward us doesn't change based on our performance, does this mean we shouldn't get into the Word? No! If we're truly born again, it's our nature to hunger for the truth.... If we're aware of the reality that we are in a battle and Satan is coming against us, then we'll realize it's to our advantage to get into the Word because it changes our hearts and corrects our attitudes. Being in God's Word gives us revelation and helps keep the devil from having access into our lives.... If you're truly born again, you desire to live holy and to minimize Satan's opportunities against you."[5]

His Word is a mirror, and if we look into the face of His Word, we can see where we are. It should give us the desire to want to improve ourselves and please Him. The Bible says we are to judge ourselves (Matt. 7:5; 1 Cor. 11:31). We are also told to keep ourselves, so the wicked one would touch us not (1 John 5:18).

The promises of God are not automatic but conditional (Gal. 3:13–14, 29; Heb. 11:6; 1 John 3:22; 3 John 2). In addition, we have to know what those promises are to appropriate them (Prov. 15:28; 2 Tim. 2:15). Hosea 4:6 says, "My people are destroyed for lack of knowledge." Proverbs 4:20–22 says to "attend to my words." We have to do the attending (Ps. 119:98–100; 2 Cor. 5:17; Phil. 3:14; James 1:21).

This comparison is not meant to condemn us but rather to better us. God's Word is the plum line. We are told to renew our mind with the washing of the water by the Word (Rom. 12:2; Eph. 4:23; 5:26; Col. 3:10; James 1:21).

If I told you I had ten million dollars hidden for you and here is the treasure map, you wouldn't feel burdened to go look for it, would you? No, you would be excited. In that same way, we are to value God's Word and apply it to our lives (Prov. 3:1–2; 4:5–8; 5:1–2; 6:23; 7:1–4; 9:10; 10:22). We are to seek after wisdom, knowledge, and understanding as hidden treasure (Prov. 2:1–6; 4:4–8; 5:1; 7:4, 8:1–5). David said he seeks after His Word as the deer pants after water. He said he loves God's commandments above gold (Ps. 119:127). Solomon said in Proverbs 8:11, "For wisdom is better than rubies; and all the things that may be desired are not to be compared to it." He said in Proverbs 20:15, "The lips of knowledge are a precious jewel."

God's Word Is a Built-In Safeguard

God's Word is holistic, and all ties together. There are built-in safety guards in His Word that cause it to work in its fullness only as a whole.

For instance, if you don't tithe, you won't prosper God's way (Mal. 3:8–9; Matt. 23:23). However, if you do tithe and do not build God's house (focus on saving souls), the money you are blessed with will have holes in the bag and run out the door (Hag. 1:5–9). If you do not have faith, you will not receive anything from God (James 1:6–7). However, if you have great faith to move mountains and have not love, it will not do you any good (1 Cor. 13:2–3). Yet, if we do all of these, but do not honor our parents, it will not go well with us (Eph. 6:2–3). If we do not put on all the armor of God, we won't be able to withstand in the evil day (Eph. 6:13). If we do not submit ourselves to God and resist the devil, he won't flee from us (James 4:7). If we don't forgive anything, Satan will get an advantage over us (2 Cor. 2:10–11). If we labor for souls but lose our zeal for the Lord, we have left our first love, and Jesus says He will remove our candlestick (Rev. 2:2–4).

Below I have listed just a few verses to give you more of a flavor of what I'm talking about. More verses are listed in Appendix A.

> Thou shalt not lend upon usury to thy brother. [No interest charged to a brother in need.]
> —Deuteronomy 23:19

> For there is no want to them that fear him.
> —Psalm 34:9

> In the days of famine they shall be satisfied. [No recession here.]
> —Psalm 37:19

> I will pay thee my vows, which my lips have uttered and my mouth has spoken when I was in trouble. [Not forgetting]
> —Psalm 66:13–14

> Fools because of their transgression, and because of their iniquities, are afflicted. [We can avoid many afflictions by not being foolish.]
> —Psalm 107:17

> Pray for the peace of Jerusalem: they shall prosper that love thee.
> —Psalm 122:6

Fear the LORD, and depart from evil. It shall be health to thy navel, and marrow to thy bones. [Be aware of what you do and see.]

—PROVERBS 3:7–8

[Seeing the harlot] till a dart strike through *his liver.* [Liver problems]

—PROVERBS 7:23, EMPHASIS ADDED

The merciful man doeth good to his own soul: but he that is cruel troubleth his own flesh. [Cruelty to anyone or any animal]

—PROVERBS 11:17

A *faithful* ambassador is health. [Being faithful brings health.]

—PROVERBS 13:17, EMPHASIS ADDED

Envy [is] the rottenness of the bones. [You will have bone problems if you envy.]

—PROVERBS 14:30, EMPHASIS ADDED

He that is *greedy* of gain troubleth his own house.

—PROVERBS 15:27, EMPHASIS ADDED

The words of a *talebearer* are wounds, they go down to the innermost parts of the belly. [Stomach problems for a gossiper]

—PROVERBS 18:8, EMPHASIS ADDED

Be not thou one of them…that are sureties for debts. [Don't be a cosigner.]

—PROVERBS 22:26

He that covereth his sins shall not prosper. [Repent quickly.]

—PROVERBS 28:13

He that giveth unto the poor shall not lack.

—PROVERBS 28:27

Rejoice ye with Jerusalem…and your *bones* shall flourish.

—ISAIAH 66:10–14, EMPHASIS ADDED

Honour thy father and thy mother…that it may be well with thee.

—EPHESIANS 6:2–3

Giving honour unto the wife…that your prayers be not hindered.

—1 PETER 3:7

Submit yourself…to God. Resist the devil, and he will flee from you.

—JAMES 4:7

Do you see how God's Word all fits together? It is our responsibility to learn all of God's precepts and do them. In Psalm 119:4, David said, "Thou hast commanded us to keep thy precepts diligently." In verse 128 of the same psalm, he says, "Therefore I esteem *all* thy precepts concerning all things to be right; and I hate every false way" (emphasis added).

CHAPTER 12

ACTIVATE THE BLESSINGS IN GOD'S WORD

O**NE OF THE** things my wife, Annette, and I do is pray and read the Bible daily. This is not to sound overspiritual, but this is necessary for anyone to have a blessed life. Psalm 119:97 says, "O how I love thy law! It is my meditation all the day." We also speak out Scripture over ourselves and trust God for His Word to take place in our lives. This takes some effort to speak them out of our mouths daily, but God instructs us to meditate in His Word day and night (Deut. 6:1–9; Josh. 1:8; 1 Tim. 4:13–15).

We must speak His Word. Mark 11:23 says, "Whosoever shall *say...*" (emphasis added). Hebrews 4:14 says, "Let us hold fast our *profession*" (emphasis added). Joel 3:10 states, "Let the weak *say*, I am strong" (emphasis added). Deuteronomy 6:7 says, "…and shalt *talk* of them [referring to God's words mentioned in verse 6] when thou sittest in thine house, and when thou walkest by the way, and when thou liest down, and when thou risest up" (emphasis added). It even goes on to say for us to place it in front of our eyes, and on our doorposts, and our gates, and on our hand. Proverbs 4:21 says, "Let them [His words] not depart from thine eyes."

Speaking out His Word and praying continuously is what we are instructed to do (Ps. 119:62, 97; 1 Thess. 5:17).

If we are trusting in God for our health, then we first ask Him. Then we speak out many of those verses that promise us healthy lives. If it's for our finances, we find God's promises for our provision. If it's for more wisdom, protection, or whatever the case, there are verses to stand on. We have to find the verses and speak them over our lives and not speak the problem. Do we truly value His Word to the point where we will expect to receive what His Word declares? Here are some more verses to give you an idea:

> But thou shalt remember the LORD thy God: for it is he that giveth thee power to get wealth, that he may establish his covenant.
> —DEUTERONOMY 8:18

> Riches and honour come of thee.
> —1 CHRONICLES 29:12

> As long as he sought the LORD, God made him to prosper.
> —2 CHRONICLES 26:5

If they obey and serve him, they shall spend their days in prosperity, and their years in pleasures.

—JOB 36:11

For thou, LORD, wilt bless the righteous; with favour wilt thou compass him about as with a shield.

—PSALM 5:12

My son, forget not my law; but let thine heart keep my commandments: For length of days, and long life, and peace, shall they add to thee.

—PROVERBS 3:1–2

He blesseth the habitation of the just.

—PROVERBS 3:33

Attend to my words....For they are life unto those that find them, and health to all their flesh.

—PROVERBS 4:20–22

For by me thy days shall be multiplied.

—PROVERBS 9:11

The fear of the LORD tendeth to life...he shall not be visited with evil.

—PROVERBS 19:23

My people shall dwell in a peaceable habitation, and in sure dwellings.

—ISAIAH 32:18

Honour thy father and thy mother...that it may be well with thee.

—EPHESIANS 6:2

> Grace be unto you, and peace, from God our Father, and from the Lord Jesus Christ.
> —PHILIPPIANS 1:2

> And the Lord shall deliver me from every evil work.
> —2 TIMOTHY 4:18

There are verses to stand on, even for the different parts that make up our body, such as our hair, teeth, eyes, skin, legs, stature, and so forth. Here are some examples:

- Deuteronomy 34:7 says, "His [Moses's] eye was not dim, nor his natural force abated." We don't confess things like our eyes are going bad as we get older, and we are just not as strong as we used to be. No, we say the opposite as in Joel 3:10, "Let the weak say, I am strong."

- Joshua 14:10–11 says, "I am this day fourscore and five years old [eighty-five]. As yet I am as strong this day as I was in the day that Moses sent me [forty-five]." Caleb is stating he felt as strong at eighty-five as he did at forty-five years old. We also declare this, since God is no respecter of persons.

- Job 11:15, 17 says, "For then shalt thou lift up thy face without spot...and thine age shall be clearer than the noonday." We declare we have clear, healthy skin.

- Solomon wrote, "His locks [hair] are bushy, and black as a raven....His eyes are as the eyes of doves by the rivers of water, washed with milk, and fitly set....His legs are like pillars of marble [strong].... Thy hair is as a flock of goats

[thick].... Thy teeth are as a flock of sheep...and
there is not one barren among them.... Thine eyes
like the fishpools in Heshbon.... This thy stature is
like to a palm tree [upright, tall and straight]" (Song
of Sol. 5:11–12, 15; 6:5–6; 7:4, 7). We declare these
verses believing in faith that we are not going to get
hunched over and decrepit as we age.

- Hebrews 1:3 says, "[The Son], upholding all things
by the word of his power..." We declare that God
upholds all things, including our health.

Using God's Word to Speak Blessing Over My Business

My wife and I truly value God's Word and love finding these
treasures. There are many verses the Lord taught me in regard
to prospering my business, such as some of what we just read. I
began to declare what His Word said about me and not how I felt.
Throughout my real estate career, I had worked a particular tract
of homes where we resided. I listed 78 percent of all the properties
that came available during that thirty-year period. I also sold
80 percent of my own listings. The average statistic is 2 percent.
In other words, the chances of selling the home you list would be
extremely rare, as there are so many agents in the MLS system. In
addition, I sold 75 percent of the other agents' listings.

These percentages are impossible without adhering to God's
principles. Ask any agent, and they will tell you that it is unheard
of and that I am probably exaggerating. But we have the records to
prove it. This is not to brag on myself, by any means, but to boast
on what the Lord has done (Jer. 9:24).

When I first started, I felt strongly impressed by the Lord to
march around the neighborhood that I was going to work once a

day for six days, and seven times on the seventh day. I did what Joshua 1:3 mentions: "Every place that the sole of your foot shall tread upon, that have I given unto you." I prayed and fasted during those seven days. When I obtained my first listing, I prayed over the file, asked the Lord for the buyer, and thanked Him every day for sending that buyer to me. I continued doing this for the entire thirty-year period. There were many other things He taught me to do, and as a result I had become the most successful agent in the area. This is all because of Him. I could never have accomplished this on my own. His Word declares that everything I would set my hand to do would prosper, and all that I undertake He would command the blessing upon me (Deut. 28).

Of course, I had to do my part and be diligent to work. I learned good work habits and developed discipline even early in life. When I was a young teen, one of my first jobs was as a busboy at a very busy restaurant located right on the ocean in Lauderdale-by-the-Sea, Florida. I used to go in an hour early to make sure my station was set up and ready to go. I stayed after hours to get ready for the next day. I didn't get paid for it, and I did this for two years. Well, I was promoted to manager of the busboys and waitresses. Not a big position, but it was for being only fifteen years old. And I got a raise. I found out that if you go the extra mile, you will never have to ask for a raise.

What Is Biblical Prosperity?

The biblical definition of prosperity is "always having all sufficiency in all things." It is God's grace abounding toward us.

> And God is able to make *all* grace abound toward you; that ye, *always* having *all* sufficiency in *all* things, may abound to *every* good work.
> —2 Corinthians 9:8, emphasis added

Having all sufficiency in all things is a guarantee if we serve Him. The mature apostle (John) wrote, "Beloved, I wish above *all* things that thou mayest prosper and be in health, even as thy soul prospereth" (3 John 2, emphasis added). He wished it above everything else.

God is not opposed to His people having prosperity, but He is *opposed to covetousness* (to lust after, excessively desirous and greedy). First Timothy 6:10–11 states, "For the love of money is the root of all evil: which while some coveted after, they have erred from the faith, and pierced themselves through with many sorrows. But thou, O man of God, flee these things; and follow after righteousness, godliness, faith, love, patience, meekness." Money is not evil, but the love of it is.

Part of our good fight of faith (v. 12) is to follow after righteousness and not to lust after money. If we will keep our focus on eternal things and serve God, His desire is for us to prosper. Prosperity only comes through obedience to His Word. There are those who think if you talk of prosperity that you are being materialistic. Yet, how hypocritical, as everyone goes to work each day to earn money and desires to pay their bills. It is usually the poor or those who are barely making it who will criticize the more affluent. I'm not saying that if you are poor, you are not spiritual. However, you may be simply unaware of God's promises to us. The poor should never be criticized but instead helped. If you are barely making it, then you cannot be a financial blessing to anyone. You would be selfish if all you cared about is your needs. You can be poor and yet have a lust for money, and you can be wealthy and have no lust whatsoever for money.

Dr. C. Thomas Anderson states, "People who work hard for barely an adequate paycheck and who get upset if it is a few dollars short are allowing that paycheck to control their lives. Even though such people might say that money doesn't matter, their behavior says otherwise. They devote great amounts of energy and time to their paycheck....God is interested in the intent of the heart. It is the love of money that is evil, not money itself."[1]

Having the Favor of God

God wants us to have influence in this world so we can bring more souls into His kingdom. The more influence we have, the more souls won. The scripture in Romans 5:17 states, "They which receive abundance of grace and of the gift of righteousness shall reign in life by one, Jesus Christ." God's desire is for us to reign in life. What does that mean?

Dr. Theo Wolmarans said, "The Greek word 'reign' in this verse is Strong's No. 936 and other translations of this word in English are: to rule, to reign in life like a king. Clearly God desires to give you tremendous influence in this life so you can influence people toward Heaven. If they aren't saved, you can influence them to salvation. If they are believers, you can encourage them to achieve greater exploits for God's Kingdom. The more influence you have, the more people you can help."[2]

It is our responsibility to appropriate all we can from the Word in order to be the most effective person we can be for His kingdom. Look at these verses, and you will see that we can have favor with God and men, but again, it is not automatic. We have to do something:

> And Jesus increased in wisdom and stature, and in favour with God and man.
>
> —LUKE 2:52

Notice, as He increased in wisdom, He found the favor.

> Let not mercy and truth forsake thee...so shalt thou find favour and good understanding.
>
> —PROVERBS 3:3

Being merciful and truthful is a condition for obtaining favor.

> Blessed is the man that heareth me, watching daily at my gates, waiting at the posts of my doors. For whoso findeth me findeth life, and shall obtain favour with the LORD.
>
> —PROVERBS 8:34–35

Again, it is being able to receive instruction.

> He that diligently seeketh good procureth favour.
>
> —PROVERBS 11:27

> Good understanding giveth favour.
>
> —PROVERBS 13:15

> The king's favour is toward a wise servant.
>
> —PROVERBS 14:35

> Whoso findeth a wife...obtaineth favour.
>
> —PROVERBS 18:22

If we "get understanding," we will find favor. How do we "get understanding"?

> Through thy precepts I get understanding.
>> —PSALM 119:104

> He that heareth reproof getteth understanding.
>> —PROVERBS 15:32

It always comes back to us being able to receive instruction from God's Word and obeying it. In addition to that I have definitely found much more favor since I met my beautiful wife (Prov. 18:22). I know it is because of her that my life has been especially blessed.

Faith

Faith is one of the most important topics in the entire Bible for these reasons:

1. Jesus will be looking for faith (Luke 18:8).

2. We walk by faith (2 Cor. 5:7).

3. We live by faith (Gal. 3:11).

4. We are saved through faith (Eph. 2:8–9).

5. We can't please God without faith (Heb. 11:6).

Everyone's faith is at a different level, and our faith needs to be exercised. We have all been given a "measure of faith" (Rom. 12:3). No one is given a greater amount. We all start off with the same amount. Where is your faith now?

1. No faith (Mark 4:40)

2. Weak in faith (Rom. 4:20)

3. Little faith (Matt. 6:30)

4. Shipwrecked faith (1 Tim. 1:19)

5. Don't know where your faith is (Luke 8:25)

6. Strong faith (Rom. 4:20)

7. Great faith (Matt. 15:28)

8. Unfeigned faith (sincere, genuine, without hypocrisy) (2 Tim. 1:5)

9. Full of faith (Acts 6:5)

Three of the ingredients of faith are as follows:

1. Love. Galatians 5:6 says, "Faith which worketh by love." First Corinthians 13:2 states, "And though I have all faith, so that I could remove mountains, and have not charity [love], I am nothing." If we have no love, our faith is void. A requirement for faith to work is for us to walk in love.

2. Patience. James 1:3 states, "That the trying of your faith worketh patience." (See also Romans 5:3; Hebrews 6:12; 10:36; James 1:4; 5:7, 10–11; 2 Peter 1:6; Revelation 3:10; 13:10.) If we have little or no patience, then we can have little or no faith. God also has all patience (Rom. 15:5; Col. 1:11; Rev. 1:9). We will have many tests to develop our patience. This is what separates the men from the boys, so

to speak. Are we committed to stay with it and
not waver (James 1:6–8), and not allow doubt to
come out of our mouths? Time proves whether we
believe God or not.

3. Works. James 2:17 says, "Even so faith, if it hath not
works, is dead, being alone." James is explaining
that if you say to the naked or poor and needy,
"Depart in peace, be ye warmed and filled...what
doth it profit?" (v. 16). If you don't give them the
money, clothes, or housing, then your faith is dead.
Your words mean nothing without your giving.
"By works was faith made perfect" (v. 22).

Faith needs to have corresponding action. Our mouth and
our actions have to show we believe it. Praying for someone who
has no food is not enough. We need to supply the food for them
also. In regard to the believing part, here is an example: Say I
needed ten thousand dollars to pay some bills, and my dad says
he will send me the money by next Friday. If I go around saying,
"I'm worried that we are not going to be able to pay these bills,
and I sure hope we get the ten thousand dollars from Dad," well,
obviously, I'm not trusting that my dad will send it. Otherwise, I
would be at rest knowing it's coming next Friday, right? We need
to be at rest, trusting God's Word will work for us.

Acts 14:9 states, "...and perceiving that he had faith to be
healed." In other words, he had enough faith. But the converse
would be, he may not have had enough faith to be healed. James
1:6 says, "But let him ask in faith, nothing wavering...for let not
that man think that he shall receive any thing of the Lord." He
just let us know we won't receive if we have any doubt.

How often many of us doubt, and then we wonder why we

haven't received? We become double minded, as in James 1:8. We use the excuse that, "It must not be God's will," rather than admit our faith may not be as developed as it should! You might say, "But Bill, you are placing condemnation on us." No, I'm simply trying to get us to see that our faith does need to be developed. We should be able to admit that we might not yet be strong in faith. When the apostles asked Jesus why they couldn't cast out a devil from a man's son, He said, "Because of your unbelief" (Matt. 17:20). He didn't pull any punches. He wasn't placing condemnation on them. He just let them know the truth. He wanted them to learn, and that is what we should be willing to do. We should be able to receive correction from His Word. In addition, we should also be willing to receive instruction or correction from our pastors and other godly people in our lives.

Charles Spurgeon said, "Get your friends to tell you your faults, or better still, welcome an enemy who will watch you keenly and sting you savagely. What a blessing such an irritating critic will be to a wise man, what an intolerable nuisance to a fool."[3]

Jesus said over and over, "Your faith hath made you whole." Look at the woman with the issue of blood in Matthew 9:20–22. What about blind Bartimaeus in Mark 10:46–52? What about the man who was let down through the roof in Mark 2:4? What about the woman from Canaan in Matthew 15:22–28? Look at the centurion in Matthew 8:5–10. And look at the story about Jairus's daughter (Mark 5:23). In each case, it was their faith that brought the healing. The woman with the issue of blood didn't even ask Him for her healing. She just said, "If I may but touch his garment, I shall be whole" (Matt. 9:21). Jesus was pleased with her faith.

I am not talking about having faith in our own faith, but it is having faith in His faith. It is by the faith *of* Him (Gal. 2:16; 3:22; Eph. 3:12; Phil. 1:27; 3:9; Col. 2:12). We are able to appropriate the blessings of God because of what Jesus has done. It is His faith that obtained the things of God for us. We simply receive them by exercising our faith in what He has done. Our faith is in trusting what He has accomplished.

God is not moved by our whining and begging. To have faith is to show we trust and rely upon Him, and we do not look at the circumstances. We simply ask Him in faith, trust Him, and thank Him for the victory. Now, it is obvious throughout the Scriptures we have to ask for things that are scriptural (1 John 5:14). That goes without saying.

So how do we acquire faith? It comes by hearing, by reading His Word, by speaking it out of our own mouths, and by listening to good teachings on the subject. There is no other way to acquire faith. Romans 10:17 says, "So then faith cometh by hearing, and hearing by the word of God." The reason the Bible says that we can't please God without faith is because God is pleased when He can bless us. His motive in being pleased is not for self-gratification. It is because He is pleased when He can give to us. God's motive is always to give. He can't bless us unless we show Him faith.

Have a Vision for Your Life

Every one of us needs to have a vision. The Bible says, "Where there is no vision, the people perish" (Prov. 29:18). Having a vision is different from setting goals—and we should do that also—but a vision is more of a spiritual direction and plan, where a goal may not be spiritual. A vision is where God is telling you what He sees you accomplishing in your life. It is usually bigger than we would think. If you find out the vision God has for you by praying, you will discover His perfect will for your life. It will be the thing that will fulfill your desires and what He has equipped you for. It will be your destiny.

Jentezen Franklin said, "When you begin to come to your vision, you can almost hear God saying, '*This* is the highest you! This is what I see you doing. This is My dream and My vision and My destiny for your life.' It will always be bigger than what you thought you could ever do or be. It will always be impossible to achieve without the continual help of the Holy Spirit. But it is not your idea in the first place. It is His. It is God's idea for you."[4]

God's Covenant With Man

One last point: God has made a covenant with Abraham, and He blessed him and made him rich (Gen. 12:2–5, 13:1–2, 6; 17:2; 24:35, 53). We are heirs of Abraham (Gal. 3:13–14). We also have what God promised him. In Deuteronomy 28, it describes in detail the blessings and the curses. It is truly an eye-opener when you see what the curse entails. Basically, it is poverty and every sickness and disease known and unknown. In other words, we do not have to be a part of those curses since we are heirs. God has redeemed us from the curse. How wonderful is that!

CHAPTER 13

PASSING THE TESTS OF LIFE

W^{E ALL GO} through tests and trials. As a matter of fact, the Bible says in Job 7:18, "That thou shouldest visit him every morning, and try him every moment." Did you hear that? Every moment we are in a test. This life is one long test to see if we obey God, the devil, or our own lusts. At the end, Christians are examined. We are rewarded for keeping God's Word, and we lose rewards for not keeping it (Matt. 16:27; 2 Cor. 5:10–11; Heb. 11:6).

Is It God, the Devil, or Me?

One of the important areas we Christians need to discern is what is a test from God, what is an attack of the devil, and what is simply our own lack of knowledge or disobedience. Sometimes the problem is due to our sin or disobedience.

> My strength faileth because of mine iniquity
> —PSALM 31:10

> Neither is there any rest in my bones because of my sin.
> —PSALM 38:3

> Fools because of their transgression, and because of their iniquities, are afflicted.
> —PSALM 107:17

> Before I was afflicted I went astray.
> —PSALM 119:67

> He that covereth his sins shall not prosper.
> —PROVERBS 28:13

> Your sins have withholden good things from you.
> —JEREMIAH 5:25

> In meekness instructing those that oppose themselves; if God peradventure will give them repentance to the acknowledging of the truth; and that they may recover themselves out of the snare of the devil, who are taken captive by him at his will.
> —2 TIMOTHY 2:25–26

That is a sobering verse. Satan can take the person who opposes the truth captive at his will. Many people want to blame God and accuse Him for the evil, not knowing it is because of their disobedience. Let's take a closer look at the three ways problems can enter our lives.

1. Lack of knowledge

Sometimes the problems we are faced with are due to a lack of knowledge. Proverbs 24:4 states, "And by knowledge shall the chambers be filled with all precious and pleasant riches." God instructs us (Isa. 48:17), but it is up to us to learn the lessons He sets before us in His Word. Therefore, having a lack of knowledge is still no excuse. We will suffer the consequences.

> Surely these are poor; they are foolish: for they know not the way of the LORD.
>
> —JEREMIAH 5:4

> My people are destroyed for a lack of knowledge.
>
> —HOSEA 4:6

> Ye ask, and receive not, because ye ask amiss, that ye may consume it upon your lusts.
>
> —JAMES 4:3

2. Demonic influence

Sometimes the problem is demonic. If you are experiencing any destruction in your life, then you know it is from the devil.

> For the Son of man is not come to destroy men's lives, but to save them.
>
> —LUKE 9:56

> Ought not this woman, being a daughter of Abraham, whom Satan hath bound, lo, these eighteen years, be loosed?
>
> —LUKE 13:16

> The thief cometh not, but for to steal, and to kill, and to destroy.
>
> —JOHN 10:10

[Jesus] went about doing good, and healing all that were oppressed of the devil.

—ACTS 10:38

Notice, healing is good, and sickness is from the devil!

To deliver such an one unto *Satan for the destruction* of the flesh, that the spirit may be saved.

—1 CORINTHIANS 5:5, EMPHASIS ADDED

Neither give place to the devil.

—EPHESIANS 4:27

Be sober, be vigilant; because your adversary the devil, as a roaring lion, walketh about *seeking whom he may devour.*

—1 PETER 5:8, EMPHASIS ADDED

For *this purpose* the Son of God was manifested, that he might *destroy* the works of the devil.

—1 JOHN 3:8, EMPHASIS ADDED

3. Tests from God

Below are some verses that show us how God tries man.

God left him, to try him, that he might know all that was in his heart.

—2 CHRONICLES 32:31

Examine me, O LORD, and prove me; try my reins and my heart.

—PSALM 26:2

For whom the LORD loveth he correcteth; even as a father the son in whom he delighteth.

—PROVERBS 3:12

The LORD trieth the hearts.

—PROVERBS 17:3

The tests are to see how we will respond. What is in our hearts? Will God find faith or doubt? Will we trust Him or trust in something else? Tests will come to see if we truly love God and are showing love to our neighbor. The tests are to develop the fruit of the Spirit.

How the Enemy Gets In

God may withdraw His hand of protection from us if we continually disobey Him, but He is not the one causing the evil or destruction. If He does withdraw His hand of protection, it is only after many warnings. At that point, the enemy will bring the destruction.

The first thing the enemy wants to do is to steal the Word of God out of our heart. In Mark 4:15, Jesus is talking about the word sown by the wayside: "But when they have heard, Satan cometh immediately, and taketh away the word that was sown in their hearts." How does he steal it? Matthew 13:19 states, "When any one heareth the word of the kingdom, and understandeth it not, then cometh the wicked one, and catcheth away that which was sown in his heart." We must have understanding or the devil can, and will, steal the Word. How do we acquire understanding?

A good understanding have all they that do his commandments.

—PSALM 111:10

Through thy precepts I get understanding.

—PSALM 119:104

The entrance of thy words giveth light; it giveth understanding.

—Psalm 119:130

He that heareth reproof getteth understanding.

—Proverbs 15:32

We gain understanding by keeping His commandments, receiving instruction, and correction. The good fight of faith is in our minds.

Notice that the devil comes to steal the Word immediately. Why so quickly? Because once we get the Word in our hearts, we become dangerous to the devil. He doesn't want us to learn that we have authority over him, that we are more than conquerors, that we are free from the curse of the law, that we can lay hands on the sick and they will recover, that we are a prosperous people (Deut. 8:18; 1 Chron. 29:12; 2 Chron. 26:5; Ps. 5:12; Mark 16:18; Luke 10:19; Rom. 8:37; Gal. 3:13). He doesn't want us prosperous in order to help spread the gospel. No, he doesn't want us to learn these things. His desire is to keep us ignorant of God's Word.

God's desire is for us to put His Word in our hearts and our mouths. The devil's desire is to take it out. The battle is in our minds. The Bible says in 2 Corinthians 10:5 that we should be "casting down imaginations." Ephesians 6:10–18 says, "Put on the whole armour of God, that ye may be able to stand against the wiles of the devil...taking the shield of faith...to quench all the fiery darts of the wicked...praying always."

We do have an enemy, and we need not be ignorant of his devices (2 Cor. 2:11). If he can steal the Word from us, he takes our faith, which is the very thing that pleases God. James 1:6–7 says, "But let him ask in faith, nothing wavering....For let not that man think he shall receive any thing of the Lord." If the devil steals the Word, it leaves us in doubt, and we will not receive anything from God. We fight the good fight of faith (1 Tim. 6:12) by casting down imaginations. We are to gird up the loins of our mind (1 Pet. 1:13).

John Paul Jackson says, "We should build ourselves up in faith, pray in the Spirit, and keep fervent our passion for God (Col. 3:5–17).... We must stand against the enemy's deceitful schemes.... We wrestle against demonic forces who capture minds and control the actions of individuals. These evil emissaries create strongholds or fortresses in the ideologies, values and actions of people around the world.... We are to quench the fiery darts of the wicked one by deflecting them, protecting ourselves with the shield of faith. We need to guard our minds against fear and unbelief.... We need to cling to God's Word, especially His promises, in order to overcome our adversary."[1]

God said in Deuteronomy 28, if we obey His Word, we will be blessed, and if we disobey, we will be cursed. It's our choice (Deut. 30:19). In Deuteronomy 11:26–28, God says, "Behold, I set before you this day a blessing and a curse; a blessing, if ye obey the commandments of the LORD your God, which I command you this day: And a curse, if ye will not obey."

It is up to us if we want to be blessed. We would be unscriptural in saying, "Well, if God wants me blessed, He will bless me, and if not, He won't." No, that is spiritual laziness. Many want to remove the requirement of obedience and sound spiritual by saying, "It's up to God." No, God doesn't bless a lack of obedience or laziness. Proverbs 13:13 says, "He that feareth the commandment shall be rewarded." Jesus said in Matthew 25:26, "Thou wicked and lazy servant..." Proverbs 12:24 says, "Work hard and become a leader; be lazy and never succeed" (TLB). (See also Proverbs 6:6–8; 10:26; 12:27; 15:19; 20:4; 24:30–34; Ecclesiastes 11:4).

Robert T. Kiyosaki mentions that his rich dad said, "If you want to change what you are you must take on your self-doubt and your laziness.... It is your self-doubt and laziness that deny you the life you want."[2]

If your lack is due to failure, do not view it as failure. Learning what *not* to do is also considered learning. Every successful person has failed many times. Proverbs 24:16 says, "For a just man falleth seven times, and rises up again." John C. Maxwell said, "Every time you face mistakes and attempt to move forward in spite of them is a test of character. There always comes a time when giving up is easier than standing up, when giving in looks more attractive than digging in. And in these moments, character may be the only thing you have to draw on to keep you going."[3]

Herbert V. Procknow said, "The fellow who never makes a mistake takes his orders from the one who does."[4]

Jentezen Franklin said, "Well-known leadership expert John Maxwell was asked how he became such a success. He answered, quoting Thomas Edison: 'I failed my way to success.' What he meant was that he learned more from the wrong things that happened in his life than he ever learned from the right things. One of the best things to learn from a seeming failure is to pick yourself up and try again."[5]

There are many tests we must pass in order for God to trust us with money. If we do not tithe (Matt. 23:23), if we do not give to the poor (Matt. 19:21), if we do not invest our money and talents wisely (Matt. 25:14–30), He will not trust us with money. The tests we all face are for us to develop the fruit of the Spirit (Gal. 5:22–23).

God Gives Warnings

God's desire is for us to listen to him and avoid some unnecessary problems.

> For God speaketh once, yea twice, yet man perceiveth it not. In a dream, in a vision of the night...then he openeth the ears of men, and sealeth their instruction...he keepeth back his soul from the pit.
>
> —JOB 33:14

> Moreover by them [thy commandments) is thy servant warned: and in keeping of them there is great reward.
>
> —PSALM 19:9–11

> I will instruct thee and teach thee in the way which thou shalt go: I will guide thee with mine eye. Be ye not as the horse, or as the mule, which have no understanding: whose mouth must be held in with bit and bridle, lest they come near unto thee.
>
> —PSALM 32:8–9

> Blessed is the man who thou chasteneth, O LORD, and teachest him out of thy law; that thou mayest give him rest from the days of adversity.
>
> —PSALM 94:12–13

> Because I have spoken unto them, but they have not heard; and I have called unto them, but they have not answered.
>
> —JEREMIAH 35:17

Notice, we are warned by His commandments, He teaches us out of His law, He speaks to us, He calls us, He gives us dreams and visions, and He tells us not to be as one who has to be forced as the horse. His desire is for us to learn from His Word, and not through pain and loss. But look at these verses that state how He will have to deal with those who refuse to learn through His Word:

> If they break my statutes, and keep not my commandments; then will I visit their transgression with the rod, and their iniquities with stripes.
>
> —PSALM 89:31–32

> When the scorner is *punished*, the simple is made wise: and when the wise is *instructed*, he receiveth knowledge.
>
> —PROVERBS 21:11, EMPHASIS ADDED

Notice it says the simple have to be punished, but the wise are instructed. They listen and learn and do not have to be punished. But those who don't listen will have to be forced.

> Behold, we put bits in the horses' mouths, that they may obey us.
>
> —JAMES 3:3

We don't have to learn the hard way. The more we spend time with Him, the easier it becomes to hear His voice, and the more we should obey.

Guarding Our Hearts

The Bible says in Proverbs 4:23, "Keep thy heart with all diligence; for out of it are the issues of life." We are told "with all diligence"! That means we are to be extremely careful to guard what goes into our hearts. Things enter through our eyes and our ears. Jesus said to be careful what you hear and see (Luke 8:18; 10:23). In Matthew 12:34–35, Jesus said, "For out of the abundance of the heart the mouth speaketh. A good man out of the good treasure of his heart bringeth forth good things." Whatever we put into our heart will come out our mouths. And if we are to expect good things, then we must put in good things. The movies we watch and the people we associate with all will impact our spiritual growth (1 Cor. 15:33; 1 Thess. 5:22; 3 John 11). We can deceive our hearts by not watching our tongue (James 1:26). We can err in our heart because we have not known God's ways (Heb. 3:10). We can have an evil heart because of unbelief (Heb. 3:12).

The best way to protect our heart is to place the Word in it. In Psalm 119:11, David states, "Thy word have I hid in mine heart, that I might not sin against thee." We want to have a pure heart (1 Tim. 1:5; 2 Tim. 2:22; 1 Pet. 1:22). Let us not pollute it.

Hearing From God

God speaks to us through His Word. The more we read, the more we will hear from Him. Jesus said in John 10:27, "My sheep hear my voice."

> I will never forget thy precepts: for *with them thou hast quickened me.*
> —PSALM 119:93, EMPHASIS ADDED

> My son, attend to my words.
> —PROVERBS 4:20

> But blessed are your eyes, for they see: and your ears, for they hear.
> —MATTHEW 13:16

> Let every man be swift to hear, slow to speak.
> —JAMES 1:19

In addition, we hear from God by praying and listening. Romans 8:16 states, "The Spirit itself beareth witness with our spirit." If we will be patient, we will hear His voice. If we are in a rush, then we probably won't. There are many days where we have much to do, and it is easy to not take the time to pray. But I have found that, if I do take the time, I will accomplish much more during the remaining hours of the day. In addition, He will work out problems that I couldn't have, or what would have taken much more time on my own.

Martin Luther said, "I have a very busy day today. I must spend not two hours, but three, in prayer."[6]

Dr. Theo Wolmarans mentions: "Every believer can have peace by spending time with the Lord every day in prayer and reading the Bible.... As a result His peace and joy will fill our hearts.... God loves us and wants to bless us, that's why He provides this guidance for us so we can stay in His will, so we can stay in His blessing and provision, and be a witness for Him.... If we don't spend time in the Word, praising Him and fellowshipping with Him, it would be like leaving home without your antenna being up. How will we have peace? We will not be able to receive direction from God. The believer who does not spend time with God in the morning will leave home with stress in his heart, confusion in his mind and will be double minded, uncertain as to what to do."[7]

> I will bless the LORD who guides me, even at night my heart instructs me.
> —PSALM 16:7, NLT

> But there is a spirit in man, and the breath of the Almighty gives him understanding.
> —JOB 32:8, NKJV

CHAPTER 14

WISDOM—DO YOU HAVE IT?

T HE *VINE'S EXPOSITORY* *Dictionary* states that *wisdom* is, "Insight into the true nature of things, the ability to discern modes of action with a view to their results."

It is the skill to use knowledge and understanding properly. In other words, it is the ability to see truth and the big picture; to know what to do and to know what will be the outcome of a matter.

The Bible states that, "The fear of the LORD is the beginning of wisdom" (Prov. 9:10). Without the fear of the Lord, we don't even have the beginning of wisdom. We might possess some knowledge, but knowledge without wisdom only "puffs up" (1 Cor. 8:1, NKJV). According to God, you cannot even have the beginning of wisdom unless you are one who fears Him. And fearing the

Lord is only the beginning. We are to continue to seek to behold His glory and be changed into the same image from glory to glory (2 Cor. 3:18). We are to gain an appreciation and stand in awe of His Word, as it is above even His name (Ps. 138:2).

Colossians 3:16 declares, "Let the word of Christ dwell in you richly in *all* wisdom" (emphasis added). As you can see from that verse alone, if His Word dwells in us, we will gain wisdom. David said in Psalm 119:98–99, "Thou through thy commandments hast made me wiser than mine enemies....I have more understanding than all my teachers: for thy testimonies are my meditation." Why was David wiser? It was because of his meditating in God's Word and obeying it.

Except for Jesus, the wisest man who ever lived was King Solomon (1 Kings 3:5–13; 4:29–30; 10:1–7, 23; 1 Chron. 29:25; 2 Chron. 1:1–12, 9:1–6, 22; Eccles. 1:13, 16; 2:12), and he said to seek after wisdom; it is the principal thing (Prov. 4:5–8, 8:1–5). Solomon was also the wealthiest man who will ever live (2 Chron. 1:12). This individual accomplished more than any other man in history. What did the most brilliant man who has ever lived say was important? After living this life of achievements, he looked back and then summed it all up in one statement. He said, "Let us hear the conclusion of the whole matter: Fear God, and keep his commandments: for this is the whole duty of man" (Eccles. 12:13)—a short but profound statement!

Yet, we find that most do not adhere to his insightful advice (Matt. 7:13–14). Why not? I believe it is because many have the erroneous idea that the Bible represents rules and restrictions, loss of freedom, and even a life of poverty. However, the Bible is not a set of rules that restrict us, but rather it is a set of principles that liberate us. It is not a book of don'ts, but rather a book involving a relationship between God and man. In this relationship, His desire is for us to discover His perfect will for our lives, to use our talents and abilities to help spread the gospel and to feed the poor. He also desires for us to enjoy our lives and to celebrate it.

In addition, the Bible is an instruction manual for life's issues. If a mechanic works on a car and never consults the manual, he will make many unnecessary mistakes. The same goes for our lives. If we do not read our manual, the Bible, we will invite *unnecessary* hardships. Adhering to God's principles only enhances our lives. Finding wisdom is more precious than rubies or fine gold (Prov. 3:14–15).

Phil Pringle said, "Wisdom is not a rulebook. She is an attitude guiding how we do life. She rewards with favour, honour and success. Wisdom is to be knowledgeable yet not proud, confident yet not arrogant, nor naïve, but not cynical either, trusting yet not gullible, believing yet proving all things, courageous yet not foolhardy, humble yet not servile, encouraging yet not flattering, profound yet relatable, appropriate, being winsome yet uncompromising, righteous yet not self-righteous, disciplined yet celebrating life, prosperous yet not miserly, generous."[1] I think that sums up the definition of wisdom pretty well.

We don't seek the wealth; we seek the wisdom. There is an earthly wisdom, and there is a godly wisdom. James 3:15 says that earthly wisdom is sensual and devilish. Godly wisdom is "first pure, then peaceable, gentle, and easy to be intreated, full of mercy and good fruits, without partiality, and without hypocrisy" (v. 17).

To obtain godly wisdom, it first takes a commitment to our Savior, and many will not make that commitment (Matt. 7:13–14). Then James 1:5 says that we can simply ask God for wisdom, and He "giveth to all men liberally."

Again God is the one who is always giving. We only have

to ask, because Jesus said, "It is your Father's good pleasure to give you the kingdom" (Luke 12:32), and wisdom is part of the kingdom (1 Cor. 1:30).

One proof you have wisdom is that you will have a desire to win souls to Christ. Proverbs 11:30 states, "He that winneth souls is wise." Charles Spurgeon said, "Soul-winning is the chief business of the Christian....It should be the main pursuit of every true believer."[2]

A wise person is also one who has a desire to understand the things of God and to have a greater knowledge of Him. (See Psalm 119:99, 127–130, 161–162; Proverbs 1:5, 2:1–6.)

There are also great benefits to those who have wisdom. Proverbs 3:13–16 states, "Happy is the man that findeth wisdom, and the man that getteth understanding....Length of days is in her right hand; and in her left hand riches and honour." How is that for a promise? Who doesn't want a long life and riches and honor? But what will you do to obtain it? Will you incline your ear, cry after her, seek for her as for hidden treasure, wait daily at her gates, and keep His Word? (See Proverbs 2:1–4; 8:1, 3, 34.)

I remember watching a TV show when I was young called *Kung Fu*. It always started with this scene where young Caine would wait outside the temple doors in hope to be granted admittance to the school. He stayed out there day after day, all day, even in the rain. Finally, one day, the master of the school opened the door. He saw his hunger and commitment and knew he was the kind of person they wanted. The same goes with God. He is looking for someone who hungers passionately after His Word.

> Blessed is the man that heareth me [wisdom], watching
> daily at my gates, waiting at the posts of my doors.
> —PROVERBS 8:34

As the hart panteth after the water brooks, so panteth my soul after thee, O God.

—PSALM 42:1

I love thy commandments above gold…my heart
standeth in awe of thy word.

—PSALM 119:127, 161

You know, many people make a lifetime commitment of discipline to win in the Olympics or be the best at their sport. They
pay a high price. Most things in life that are worth acquiring take
discipline, persistence, and dedication. Yet most will not pay the
price for the most valuable of all pursuits. King Solomon asked
for wisdom and pursued it, and not only did God give him the
wisdom, but also wealth came along with it. That is why Proverbs
4:7 says, "Wisdom is the principal thing; therefore get wisdom:
and with all thy getting get understanding."

Another example of wisdom would be in knowing when,
what, and how to answer a matter. If what you say is delivered
with a caring attitude, instead of a haughty, corrective attitude,
it will be much more readily accepted. Also, the timing of when
something is said is crucial.

A word fitly spoken is like apples of gold in pictures
of silver.

—PROVERBS 25:11

A fool uttereth all his mind.

—PROVERBS 29:11

A wise man's heart discerneth both time and
judgment.

—ECCLESIASTES 8:5

These next stories reveal wisdom in some aspect, especially those involving Jesus.

Daniel's Attitude in a Request

In Daniel 1, Daniel and his three friends were told to eat the king's food in order to fatten themselves up before their appearance with the king. Since they had been in prison, they would, of course, not have been eating too well. The prince of the eunuchs was required to be sure they were, in fact, fattened up, or he would lose his head (v. 10). However, Daniel didn't want to defile himself with the king's food and purposed himself not to eat it. He decided to ask if he could eat only vegetables. He had to ask with wisdom, as the man would normally say, "Not even a possibility." Daniel said to the prince, "Prove thy servants, I beseech thee, ten days; and let them give us pulse [vegetables] to eat, and water to drink" (v. 12).

Two points I want to make: First of all, he asked for only a ten-day trial run, which would still leave enough time for the king's food to be given if Daniel's way of eating only vegetables didn't work. This would have been in the mind of the prince, since he didn't want to lose his head. Daniel showed consideration of him by asking for only the ten days. The prince had three years to fatten them up (v. 5). Daniel also had to have been in a favorable position with the prince of the eunuchs to even ask in the first place (v. 9). This was due to him having an excellent spirit (Dan. 5:12, 14; 6:3).

The second thing to notice in Daniel's asking is that he said, "I beseech thee..." *Beseech* means "please" or "I beg you." The attitude was not insistent in any way, but instead humble. All through the Bible the word *beseech* is used by those with a humble attitude. Daniel asked the Lord and said, "I beseech thee..." (Dan.

9:16). Paul said in 2 Corinthians 10:1, "Now I Paul myself beseech you by the meekness and gentleness of Christ, who in presence am base among you." Daniel asked with wisdom, and he was granted his request. Consideration of others is showing wisdom.

> A man shall be satisfied with good by the fruit of his mouth.
>
> —PROVERBS 12:14

> A soft answer turns away wrath: but grievous words stir up anger. The tongue of the wise useth knowledge aright.
>
> —PROVERBS 15:1–2

> Kindness makes a man attractive.
>
> —PROVERBS 19:22, TLB

Wisdom in Confrontation

This is an excellent story of just how to say something in order for it to be received well. Look at the situation where the prophet Nathan had to tell King David about his sin with Bathsheba. Instead of telling him straight on, he told him a story that is recorded in 2 Samuel 12:1–7:

> There were two men in one city; the one rich, and the other poor. The rich man had exceeding many flocks and herds: But the poor man had nothing, save one little ewe lamb, which he had bought and nourished up: and it grew up together with him, and with his children; it did eat of his own meat, and drank of his own cup, and lay in his bosom, and was unto him as a daughter. And there came a traveller unto the rich man, and he spared to take of his

121

own flock and of his own herd, to dress for the way-faring man that was come unto him; but took the poor man's lamb, and dressed it for the man that was come to him. And David's anger was greatly kindled against the man; and he said to Nathan, As the LORD liveth, the man that hath done this thing shall surely die.... And Nathan said to David, Thou art the man.

You can see how David would have now been convicted and couldn't brush it off. It would not have been an easy thing to simply walk up to the king and tell him he was in sin, even as a prophet. It took the wisdom of God, and David's heart was convicted to repent.

The story of Esther is the most amazing display of God's wisdom in operation. There are too many points to emphasize here, so I encourage you to read the account. It is a marvelous example of how prayer and fasting will bring God on the scene. You will also see how He is well able to reverse some disastrous events from occurring and to see that justice takes place.

The Answers of Jesus

Who will cast a stone?

I want to share a few stories of the One who has the ultimate wisdom—Jesus Christ.

In John 8, there was a situation where the scribes and Pharisees brought a woman to Jesus who was caught in adultery. They reminded Jesus that "Moses in the law commanded us, that such should be stoned: but what sayest thou?" (v. 5). The Law said she should be stoned, and they were right. So how would Jesus show mercy to her but not violate His own Word? His ministry was to fulfill the Law, but Jesus always showed mercy to the humble, and He showed forgiveness. How could He accomplish both?

He looked at all those hypocrites who were accusing her and stooped down to write in the sand. Then He stood up and said, "He that is without sin among you, let him first cast a stone at her" (v. 7). His answer did not violate His established Word, but at the same time, it rose above the Law and brought mercy and forgiveness.

With the statement Jesus made, there was no way those men could demand that the Law be carried out. Their guilt left them speechless. It positioned her for mercy. What a display of the wisdom of God in not violating His own Word and yet rising above it. Scholars speculate that He was probably writing their sins on the ground. Those scoundrels were accusing her, when they were worse (Matt. 23:13–33). He shut their mouths. God's awesome wisdom and His obvious disdain for hypocrisy is something to shout about.

Show me a penny!

There was another incident in Mark 12:14–17, where the Pharisees and the Herodians asked Jesus, "Is it lawful to give tribute to Caesar, or not?" They knew that most of the crowd were Jews and didn't like having to pay taxes. If Jesus said to pay it, the crowd would hate Him and not listen to His Words. If He told them not to pay it, He could be arrested by the Roman government for promoting tax evasion. They wanted to trap Him, but they didn't know whom they were playing with. Jesus said the famous line, "Render to Caesar the things that are Caesar's, and to God the things that are God's." He didn't break the law regarding the payment of taxes, but He didn't let those hypocritical religious leaders off the hook either. They themselves were not giving the way they were commanded to in the Scriptures (Matt. 23:14), such as helping and giving to the poor (Matt. 23:2–4). He let them know in a subtle way that they were not so pious. The Jews could more readily accept His statement to pay the taxes now since He showed them His command to also give to God, as they would have agreed.

By what authority?

In Matthew 21:23–27, "The chief priests and the elders…said, 'By what authority doest thou these things? and who gave thee this authority?' And Jesus answered and said unto them, I also will ask you one thing, which if ye tell me, I in like wise will tell you by what authority I do these things. The baptism of John, whence was it? from heaven, or of men? And they reasoned with themselves, saying, If we shall say, From heaven; he will say unto us, Why did ye not then believe him? But if we shall say, Of men; we fear the people; for all hold John as a prophet. And they answered Jesus, and said, We cannot tell. And he said unto them, Neither tell I you by what authority I do these things."

These religious leaders tried to trap Him, and He in turn stopped their mouths. Again, the wisdom of God is astounding! There are many more stories throughout the Bible that reveal wisdom on how, when, and in what attitude to say a thing.

Wisdom From Wise Association

Proverbs 13:20 states that, "He that walketh with wise men shall be wise: but a companion of fools shall be destroyed." We can pick up the spirit of wisdom as we associate with wise people and as we stay connected to our all-wise God. Wisdom doesn't come by casual contact. The verse says, "He that walketh…"; that means, day in and day out spending time with those who are wise.

We could look at the relationship of Moses and Joshua. Joshua served Moses for forty years and had a similar anointing as Moses. Deuteronomy 34:9 says, "And Joshua the son of Nun was full of the spirit of wisdom; for Moses had laid his hands upon him." Look at Elijah and Elisha. Scholars say Elisha served Elijah for between ten and twenty years. Then Elisha had twice the miracles as Elijah (2 Kings 2:9–15). Look at Paul and Timothy. They served together in the ministry, and Timothy benefited from Paul's insight. Paul said Timothy was his "dearly beloved son…the unfeigned faith that is in thee" (2 Tim. 1:2, 5).

We should be desirous of an opportunity where God may arrange for us to be divinely connected to someone. Those relationships are extremely beneficial for us. We should choose our friends wisely and be aware of divine connections.

Wisdom is also knowing who you are dealing with and how to handle different people. There are three different types of people in the world, according to Dr. Henry Cloud: "Wise people, foolish people, evil people. Those are the three categories of behavior that you will find yourself dealing with in virtually any situation involving others.…Different people, in different categories, require different strategies."[3] Just as there is a weather satellite to predict the weather, there is a way to predict people. He states, "The satellite that will give you the most accurate predictions is the ability to diagnose character."[4]

We must understand what the character of the person is so we know how to deal with them. You don't handle everyone the same way that works for you. Dr. Cloud points out that the key diagnostic of the wise person is: "When truth presents itself, the wise person sees the light, takes it in, and makes adjustments.…The mature person meets the demands of life, while the immature person demands that life meet her demands.…Wise people likewise address their faults, and you see changes in actions and behaviors instead of patterns that go unaffected by the feedback.... The fool does the opposite: he rejects the feedback, resists it, explains it away, and does nothing to adjust to meet its requirements." He goes on to explain evil people, "There are some people whose desire is to hurt others and do destructive things.... This is difficult for some leaders to come to grips with; they think that they can reason with anyone and finally get through. But evil people are not reasonable. They seek to destroy. So you have to protect yourself—ergo, lawyers, guns (police), and money."[5] He summarizes the three:

1. With wise people—Talk to them, give resources, and you will get a return.

2. With foolish people—Stop talking to them about problems; they are not listening. And stop supplying resources; they squander them. Instead, give them limits and consequences.

3. With evil people—You have to go into protection mode, not helping mode, when dealing with evil people.[6]

Here is the key to obtaining wisdom and knowledge:

The LORD is exalted; for he dwelleth on high: he hath filled Zion with judgment and righteousness. And wisdom and knowledge shall be the stability of thy times, and strength of salvation: the fear of the LORD is his treasure.

—ISAIAH 33:5–6

Did you get that? The fear of the Lord is our treasure. He let us know one of the keys of life. Reverential fear is the foundation of wisdom and knowledge.

> Surely his salvation is nigh them that fear him.
> —PSALM 85:9

> The fear of the LORD is the beginning of knowledge.
> —PROVERBS 1:7

> The fear of the LORD is the beginning of wisdom.
> —PROVERBS 9:10

If we don't fear Him, we will not be able to grasp the wisdom and knowledge of Him, and of salvation. Finding a key is like discovering buried treasure as Proverbs 2:4 states. Then Solomon said, "[Wisdom] is more precious than rubies: and all the things thou canst desire are not to be compared unto her.... She is a tree of life.... My fruit is better than gold" (Prov. 3:15, 18; 8:19).

Another interesting verse is Proverbs 11:12. It states, "He that is void of wisdom despiseth his neighbour." If we don't show love, like the story Jesus told about the Good Samaritan, we would be despising our neighbor. That would cause us to be void of wisdom. I had not connected the fact that how I treat my neighbor would affect my possessing wisdom or to be void of it.

Proverbs 2 says to seek after wisdom, knowledge, and understanding. We need all three. We gave the definition of wisdom at the beginning of this chapter. Let's look at knowledge and understanding.

According to *Vine's*, *knowledge* is "Seeking to know—investigate—gather information, Not merely intellectual activity, but by the Holy Ghost." How do we get knowledge?

The fear of the LORD is the beginning of knowledge:
but fools despise wisdom and instruction.

—PROVERBS 1:7

If thou seekest her [wisdom] as silver, and searchest
for her as for hid treasure; then thou shalt...find the
knowledge of God.

—PROVERBS 2:4–5

Whoso loveth instruction loveth knowledge.

—PROVERBS 12:1

The heart of the prudent getteth knowledge.

—PROVERBS 18:15

He giveth wisdom unto the wise, and knowledge to
them that know understanding.

—DANIEL 2:21

If you have understanding, you are given knowledge.
Vine's says that *understanding* means to "bring together—to set
together—fully perceived." How do we receive understanding?

A good understanding have all they that *do* his
commandments.

—PSALM 111:10, EMPHASIS ADDED

Through thy *precepts* I get understanding, therefore
I hate every false way.

—PSALM 119:104, EMPHASIS ADDED

Here is a short list of the characteristics of a person with
wisdom, knowledge, and understanding:

Wisdom	Knowledge	Understanding
Fears the Lord (Prov. 9:10)	Slow to speak (Prov. 17:27)	Takes correction (Prov. 15:32)
Hates evil (Prov. 8:13)	Conceals knowledge (Prov. 12:23)	Holds his temper (Prov. 11:12)
Wins souls (Prov. 11:30)	Is disciplined (Prov. 12:1)	Slow to wrath (Prov. 14:29)
Guards his mouth (Prov. 16:23)	Doesn't brag (Prov. 12:23)	Seeks good (Prov. 11:27)
Has wise advisors (Prov. 13:10)	Is strong (Prov. 24:5)	No vain friends (Prov. 12:11)
Is humble (Prov. 11:2)	Is wealthy (Prov. 24:4)	Walks uprightly (Prov. 15:21)
Is discreet (Prov. 5:2)	Overlooks insults (Prov. 12:16)	Has favor (Prov. 13:15)
Is patient (Prov. 14:29)	Retains riches (Prov. 11:16)	Has an excellent spirit (Prov. 17:27)
Not quick to judge (Prov. 29:11)	Covers shame (Prov. 12:16)	Is preserved (Prov. 4:6)
Speaks after hearing (Prov. 29:11)	Is prudent (Prov. 14:18)	Doesn't cosign (Prov. 17:18)

Fearing God is only the beginning. We are to grow to hate evil and to desire to see His beauty and to be in His presence (Ps. 27:4).

Wisdom is necessary for having answers to help guide us in our walk. In addition, it enables us to have answers for people, especially if you are a leader (2 Chron. 1:11). It is for the purpose to help influence people to the Lord (Prov. 11:30). In addition, it is for us to be better at our jobs. Exodus 36:1 says, "In whom the LORD put wisdom and understanding, to know how to work all manner of work for the service of the sanctuary." This was to perform work on the house of the Lord. However, I believe it is also for us to be more skillful in any work, in order to reflect the excellence of the Lord in us.

> And they came, every one whose heart stirred him up, and every one whom his spirit made willing.... And all the women that were wise hearted... and all the women whose heart stirred them up in wisdom.
>
> —EXODUS 35:21, 25–26

> And all the wise men, that wrought all the work of the sanctuary.
>
> —EXODUS 36:4

> And he was filled with wisdom, and understanding, and cunning to work all works in brass.
>
> —1 KINGS 7:14

> [David] guided them [Israel] by the skillfulness of his hands.
>
> —PSALM 78:72

> God gave them knowledge and skill in all learning and wisdom.
>
> —DANIEL 1:17

> An excellent spirit was in him.
>
> —DANIEL 6:3

For further study, read: Exodus 36:1; 1 Chronicles 5:18, 22; 28:21; 2 Chronicles 1:11–12; 2:14; Nehemiah 2:18; 4:6; Psalm 33:3; Proverbs 1:2–5; Ecclesiastes 12:9; Colossians 4:6; 1 Peter 3:15.

As you can see, if we have a willing heart and a spirit that we stir up ourselves to work, then God gives us the wisdom, knowledge, and skill to do a better job. Our attitude makes the difference. Daniel 2:21 states, "He giveth wisdom unto the wise." The wise are those who fear Him (Prov. 9:10).

I would like to share a dream I had from the Lord that revealed a part of the wisdom I needed to prosper.

CHAPTER 15

GOD'S WISDOM REVEALED

O NE NIGHT I had a dream, and this dream was different from the usual dreaming we all have. I knew that it was from God, and I have never forgotten it. Most of us, at some point, have received a dream from God, even if we didn't realize it (Job 33; Joel 2:28).

In this dream, I was in my home, and I suddenly could see right through the walls. I saw this big snake, and it was pounding on the walls and windows trying to get in. It was fat, approximately a foot in diameter, slimy, and green in color. It was relentless in its attempts to find an opening. I had felt that it could not see. It was trying to find an opening by its mere pounding all around the house. There were no windows opened, and all was closed up.

However, I looked over to our front door and it appeared to have been sawn short. It didn't come down to the floor. It was as if someone sawed the bottom six or eight inches off. I became fearful, as I knew eventually this snake would find the opening and get in. About a half an hour passed in the dream, and sure enough the snake hit the opening and then squeezed under the bottom of the door. It began tearing up the house, and its slime was getting on everything. I became frightened and ran out the back door. Once outside I thought, "I need to go back in and get that thing out of my house." I proceeded back in, and then I woke up.

I was certain this dream was from God, and it really concerned me. I asked the Lord to give me the interpretation of its meaning. I prayed for a while, and then I got it. I did not hear an audible voice, but I felt strongly impressed and had the understanding so clearly. In addition, there was a peace that came over me with this understanding.

The interpretation was this: Of course the snake was a demonic spirit. That part is obvious. It was attempting to get into my life, as the house represented my life. He couldn't see that there were walls, but he knew enough to continue to pound to eventually find an opening. The walls represented the hedge that is around our lives if we live for the Lord and are saved.

Jesus gave a parable in Mark 12 and said, "A certain man planted a vineyard, and set an hedge about it..." (v. 1). We know the man in the parable is God, and the vineyard was Israel.[1] God had set a hedge around Israel, and He has set one around us. Ecclesiastes 10:8 says, "Whoso breaketh an hedge, a serpent shall bite him." In Job 1:10, Satan said to God, "Hast not thou made an hedge about him, and about his house, and about all that he hath on every side?" So we have a hedge, but we can break it ourselves.

My hedge was obviously open, and at the front door. Now, the front door represented the first thing that would give entry into my life, which was praying and reading God's Word on a daily basis. In other words, the first thing we are to do every morning is worship Him, pray, and read His Word. In Mark 1:35 it states that Jesus "rising up a great while before day, he went out, and departed into a solitary place, and there prayed." Ezekiel 12:8 states, "In the morning came the word of the LORD unto me." There are many other verses which state this. (See Deuteronomy 6:8; Job 7:17–18; Psalm 5:3; 57:8; 59:16; 63:1; 78:34; 108:2; Jeremiah 25:3.)

Our reading and praying first thing of the day shows God that He has the first place in our lives. Well, I would miss a day here and there, but each day I missed, the crack under the front door grew larger. My hedge was beginning to open. God can also remove it if we are in disobedience (Ps. 80:12; 89:40; Isa. 5:5; Mark 12:1). This open hedge invited problems into my life, and it was my fault.

Prior to my dream, there was this one particular day that I was at the gym, and someone bumped the weight rack and a five-pound weight fell and hit my big toe. It broke my toe! It was the only time in my life I have broken a bone. It really hurt. I had complained to the Lord and said, "Why did this happen? Your Word says no evil shall happen to the just." (See Psalms 54:7; 121:7; Proverbs 11:8; 12:21; 19:23; Ecclesiastes 8:5.) Then, just days later, I had that dream.

I believe the Lord said to me, after He told me the interpretation of the dream, "You had time to go to the gym every day, but not time to pray and read My Word every day." Now God is not the one who caused that weight to fall on my toe. However, we do have an enemy, and there are benefits when we stay under the umbrella of God's protection. I gave place to the devil, and the

Bible tells us not to (Eph. 4:27). His Word declares that we can be hidden in the secret place, that no evil shall befall us, that we shall not be visited with evil, wickedness shall not afflict us, that not a bone shall be broken, that the enemy shall flee seven ways before us, and so on (Deut. 28:7; Ps. 27:5; 31:20; 34:20; 89:22; 91:1; Prov. 12:21; 19:23). I believe God made it clear to me to read and pray daily as He said in Deuteronomy 6:1–9, Joshua 1:8, and elsewhere.

Now, some have said to me, "Bill, you are in legalism. You are in bondage. It's legalistic to say we must read and pray daily. You are on a works trip." I understand their thoughts. We can go too far, and no one can keep all the Word. I also know that the New Testament says that if we are in works, then we are not under grace. However, our reason for wanting to keep His Word is out of a desire to please Him, not out of works to earn anything. We are to be doers of the Word. This is also not a works trip because it does not have to do with my salvation but with my protection. Look at these three verses:

> O how I love thy law! It is my meditation all the day.
> —PSALM 119:97

> Thank we God without ceasing.
> —1 THESSALONIANS 2:13

> Pray without ceasing.
> —1 THESSALONIANS 5:17

How many of us do that?

If we are told to pray and give thanks without ceasing and to meditate on His Word all day, then why is it legalism to read and pray daily? The Word is clear that we are to stay in obedience if we want the blessings and promises of God (Josh. 1:8; Job 36:11; Ps.

1:1; 37:19; 122:6; Prov. 3:33; 4:5–8; 22:4; 24:4; Eccles. 8:5; Isa. 1:19; Jer. 5:25; Luke 6:35–38; Heb. 11:6; 1 John 3:22).

Hebrews 11:6 states, "He is a rewarder of them that diligently seek him."

You become legalistic when you think that you are earning your blessings. God gives us the grace to keep His Word and overcome sin. It is not that I feel justified in walking in the blessings because of *keeping* His Word. It is because I desire to show Him I love Him by *obeying* His Word.

I'm sure we all eat food and drink every day, even three times a day. Now would I be justified in saying you were being fanatical for eating every day? Yet Jesus said that His Word is our daily bread (Luke 11:3; John 6:33, 41, 48). He said that man does not live by bread alone but by every Word of God. Reading and praying daily is more important than eating food. It is, again, another place in His Word to obey and see the benefits.

I'm simply sharing what has worked in my life. I have done this for thirty-two years since the dream, and He has protected my wife and me faithfully. I have been kept healthy and not had any sick days or any injuries. It is not because of what we have done, but because He is faithful to keep His Word. Our part is simply to obey and give Him thanks every day (Ps. 61:8; 72:15; 86:3; 119:164; Acts 17:11; 1 Cor. 15:31; 1 John 3:22).

Proverbs 8:34 says, "Blessed is the man that heareth me [wisdom], watching *daily* at my gates, waiting at the posts of my doors" (emphasis added).

Wisdom—Seeing the End Result

My brother-in-law Greg is a corporate CPA and also advises wealthy clients in their investments. One of his clients had purchased this land to develop a shopping center, hotel, office buildings, and so forth. After a year of research, the team of attorneys and he had completed their feasibility study and all reports as to the profitability. They were all assembled and decided it was a go. Greg informed the owner that he would earn in profits approximately ten million dollars after one year of operation. It would be a very successful venture. They were all prepared to proceed ahead, then Greg pulled the owner aside to make this comment: "Mike, you will make ten million, but you are seventy years old, and the project will take five years out of your life. You might not have much longer after that to even enjoy the money, and you already have hundreds of millions. Why not just enjoy these later years with your wife."

Mike decided Greg was right, and they canceled the project. Now Greg would have earned half a million for his part in just the first year alone. But instead of thinking of himself, he thought of Mike and saw the big picture.

The advice to Mike was, first, wisdom on Greg's part, and second, it reflected the love of God to look out for others even at your own expense. Yes, that is the Golden Rule, which many do not fully understand or follow. John C. Maxwell states, "To many people, the Golden Rule sounds like a soft approach to business. But nothing could be further from the truth.... It really is a win for everybody.... The Golden Rule really does work."[2]

Often, our self-centered lives take precedence over another's needs, and we fail to comprehend that this Golden Rule is actually the law of sowing and reaping. How we treat others will come back on us in this life and in the life to come.

Greg has not focused on the money. He has been very blessed and prosperous during his entire career. This is also due to his wife, his better half, Janice. Greg, like me, also married over his head! Seeing the end result *is* godly wisdom.

Wisdom Reveals the Answer

I had sold a home, and we were about one month into the escrow. The preliminary title report showed that the owner had a second trust deed of $100,000 on the property. However, they had told me that it had been paid off fourteen years earlier. However, the payoff of $100,000 was never recorded. The escrow company at that time should have recorded a Reconveyance Deed, which is a document used to show the loan was paid off. Well, they didn't, so it still showed as owed. The next place to go would be the old escrow company to see if they had any old records, but they had closed years ago. Then we went to the title company to check with them, but they had been bought out by another. So we went to that company, and they were out of business. We tracked it to seven different companies, and all were long gone. So our current title company did not want to insure the title unless we could prove it had been paid. The owner couldn't find the old file or any old monthly bills received from the lender, which would have showed the decreasing balance. They were searching for anything that could show the payments were made. The title company did not want to insure it no matter what alternative documents they could find. We tried two more title companies, and they also said no. I knew to pray for wisdom, as God would tell me what to do next.

I asked the seller if they could search for any canceled checks. They had been looking for anything to do with the loan but hadn't found a thing. They finally found a check made payable to the bank that the loan had been with. It was for the amount of their old payment. It was dated only one month prior to when they said the loan had been paid off. The footnote on the check said "last payment."

Now I thought, "If we would do a credit report on them, then perhaps this $100,000 loan would show up as paid, and at that date." Many times old loans that had been paid off would drop off your credit report after ten years. So I didn't know if it would show or not. Well, it did and showed "paid," and the date showed one month after their check that showed "last payment." The payment amount on the credit report matched the amount on their check. I also had them get all their current checking accounts statements that reflected all their monthly payments. None of them showed any amount being paid for a second trust deed payment. If the second still existed, and they had not been making any payments due for over fourteen years, then there would have been a notice of default filed by someone. It would have shown up on the title report, and also it would reflect on their credit report. Of course, there wasn't any. With these three items, and a letter from them stating that it had been paid in full, I felt it would be enough to convince the title company to insure the title, even though they said they would not take any alternative documentation.

We talked to a manager at the title company and explained, and they agreed that it was enough but would still insure around it and list it as an exception. That was good enough for the buyer. The escrow closed after a two-month delay. Even though the title company had stated they wouldn't consider any alternative documentation, I felt led to pursue it. I was prompted by the Lord to think of those items needed, and He also gave us the favor with the title company. Many times you simply can't take no for an answer. Persistence and being determined will prevail.

The hand of the diligent maketh rich.

—PROVERBS 10:4

The soul of the sluggard desireth, and hath nothing:
but the soul of the diligent shall be made fat.

—PROVERBS 13:4

Foresight

A friend of mine, who was also a real estate broker, had been
working for a builder at the time the market was really coming
to a standstill. She held the highest position and was the highest-
paid employee. She understood that since everyone was getting
laid off, her time would come also. Instead of waiting for her
bosses to come to her and have to let her go, she decided to go
to them. She told them that they couldn't afford to pay her what
she had been making but could only afford one-half of her salary.
They were shocked that she was advising them to cut her salary in
half. Proverbs 27:12 states, "A prudent man foreseeth the evil, and
hideth himself; but the simple pass on, and are punished."

They respected her honesty and kept her on board, taking
her advice. Now, if she wouldn't have gone to them, they would
have let her go, and she would have had no income. It was almost
impossible to find a job, as everyone was laying people off. Her
plan kept her at her job. To coin a phrase from the Bible, she saw
that the "handwriting was on the wall." (See Daniel 5:5.)

After the economy recovered, guess whom they gave a raise
to, and placed her at even higher than before. Would you have
recommended your company cut your salary in half? Wisdom is
seeing the end result.

CHAPTER 16

THE POWER OF HUMILITY

J ESUS IS OUR supreme example of a humble person. We will look at His life just ahead.

But first, many think that a humble person is someone who does not stand up for himself or is passive and has no worldly possessions. Being poor is often viewed as being humble. Yet, this is completely unbiblical. So what is a truly humble person like? What are his characteristics? How does humility affect our prospering?

King Solomon states in Proverbs 22:4, "By humility and the fear of the LORD are riches, and honour, and life." A humble person in God's eyes is someone who prays and fasts. It is someone with a contrite spirit (feeling or showing sorrow and remorse for sin or shortcoming). (See 2 Kings 22:19; Psalms 34:18; 51:17; Isaiah

57:15; 66:2.) This is not someone who lacks confidence but rather is confident because of what Jesus has done for them. Proverbs 14:26 states, "In the fear of the LORD is strong confidence." (See also 2 Thessalonians 3:4; Hebrews 3:6; 10:35; 1 John 2:28.)

A truly humble person is neither haughty in any way nor demanding or condescending. However, he is also not weak or passive. He is direct and strong yet shows love and consideration for everyone.

The life of Jesus would, of course, reflect the characteristics of a humble person. What was Jesus like? The Bible shows that He is purposed, yet not forceful; He is uncompromised, yet not demanding. He is forthright, yet not inconsiderate; He speaks with infinite wisdom, yet not condescending. He is kind, yet without partiality; He always displays love, yet without conditions. He never softened His message in order to be liked or accepted. He simply stated the truth. His message was clear. He said, "I am the way, the truth, and the life: no man cometh unto the Father, but by me" (John 14:6). He said, "I came...to save the world" (John 12:47). He said in John 8:24, "If ye believe not that I am he [the Savior], ye shall die in your sins." He said in John 11:25, "I am the resurrection, and the life: he that believeth in me, though he were dead, yet shall he live. And whosoever liveth and believeth in me shall never die." In John 10:30 and 36 Jesus said, "I and my Father are one....I am the Son of God." His message was uncompromising, because He spoke truth.

What did Jesus preach? He preached repentance, obedience, forgiveness, and kindness. He preached "to love thy God with all thy heart...and thy neighbour as thyself" (Luke 10:27). The very first recorded word out of the mouth of Jesus at the start of His ministry was *repent* (Matt. 4:17). Repentance requires humility. It is saying, "I need forgiveness." In 2 Corinthians 7:9, Paul mentions being sorrowed to repentance. Psalm 34:18 says, "The LORD is nigh unto them that are of a broken heart; and saveth such as be of a contrite spirit."

Jesus also preached for people to obey. He said, "My mother and my brethren are these which hear the word of God, and do it" (Luke 8:21). (See also Matthew 7:21; 12:50; Luke 8:21; 1 John 2:3, 17). Obedience is another characteristic of humility. Even Jesus showed obedience. Philippians 2:8 says, "And being found in fashion as a man, he humbled himself, and became obedient unto death, even the death of the cross." Hebrews 5:8 states, "Though he were a Son, yet learned he obedience by the things he suffered." Psalm 113:6 reads, "Who [the Lord] humbleth himself to behold the things that are in heaven, and in the earth!" If the Creator of the entire universe can show obedience to the Father, then who are we to do otherwise? Our obedience demonstrates we are submitted to authority, which reflects humility. Jesus also taught us obedience because it is for our benefit. Obedience keeps us from evil (Deut. 28). This is why He is strong about warning us to avoid sin. He let people know and wants them to understand the consequences of sin. He didn't say, "Oh, that's all right. I know you've been hurt. Just be yourself." No, He called sin a sin. Being soft on sin isn't showing humility. Being straightforward and speaking truth *is*.

He told the man at the pool of Bethesda to "sin no more, lest a worse thing come unto thee" (John 5:14). He told Mary Magdalene to "go and sin no more" (John 8:11). He said, "Your sins are forgiven" (Matt. 9:2, 5–6; Mark 2:5, 9–10; Luke 5:20, 23–24; 7:48). He wasn't concerned about being politically correct.

He called the religious leaders of His day hypocrites, fools, blind, full of extortion and excess, full of dead men's bones, whited sepulchers, full of iniquity, serpents, and a generation of vipers (Matt. 23:13–33). These religious leaders were of the worst lot, as they led people to believe that God was harsh with so many rules. And the fact was they themselves didn't follow all those rules (Matt. 23:3–5, 14; Luke 11:46). Many of the rules were self-imposed and not from God. They didn't show any love to anyone but themselves. Jesus said in Matthew 23:13–15, "For ye shut up the kingdom of heaven against men: for ye neither go in yourselves, neither suffer ye them that are entering to go in.... Ye devour widows' houses, and for a pretence make long prayer...for ye compass sea and land to make one proselyte, and when he is made, ye make him twofold more the child of hell than yourselves."

Jesus stood up to them and told them the truth. He never compromised. A humble person is one who doesn't allow injustice to go unchallenged. Proverbs 28:4 states, "They that forsake the law praise the wicked: but such as keep the law *contend* with them" (emphasis added). Psalm 89:8 reads, "O Lord God of hosts, who is a strong Lord like unto thee?" David said in Psalm 119:104, "I hate every false way."

A humble person is one who doesn't think too highly of himself (Rom. 12:3) and doesn't demand special treatment. Paul said in Philippians 4:12, "I know both how to be abased, and I know how to abound." Donald Gray Barnhouse says, "Christ sends none away empty but those who are full of themselves."[1]

Jesus tells a story in Luke 18:10–14 where He says, "Two men went up into the temple to pray; the one a Pharisee, and the other a publican. The Pharisee stood and prayed thus with himself, God, I thank thee, that I am not as other men are, extortioners, unjust, adulterers, or even as this publican. I fast twice in the week, I give tithes of all that I possess. And the publican standing afar off, would not lift up so much as his eyes unto heaven, but smote upon his breast, saying, God be merciful to me a sinner. I tell you, this man went down to his house justified rather than the other: for every one that exalts himself shall be abased; and he that humbleth himself shall be exalted."

You see, Pharisees were the religious leaders and the educated of the day, where publicans were considered the outcasts and uneducated. God judges by the heart and not the outward appearance, status, or culture.

Another story from Jesus in Luke 14:8–10 states, "When thou art bidden of any man to a wedding, sit not down in the highest room; lest a more honorable man than thou be bidden of him; and he that bade thee and him come and say to thee, Give this man place; and thou begin with shame to take the lowest room. But when thou art bidden, go and sit down in the lowest room; that when he that bade thee cometh, he may say unto thee, Friend, go up higher: then shalt thou have worship in the presence of them that sit at meat with thee."

Proverbs 15:33 states, "Before honour is humility." If you humble yourself, God will exalt you (James 4:10). James 3:13 states, "Who is there among you who is wise and intelligent? Then let him by his noble living show forth his [good] works with the [unobtrusive] humility [which is the proper attribute] of true wisdom" (AMP).

Be Zealous for God

Another important characteristic of humility is "passion" or "zeal." How does this reflect humility? Being zealous toward God shows we are placing Him first in our lives, as zeal means you are consumed with His purposes. David said, "My zeal hath consumed me" (Ps. 119:139).

Placing Him first means you yourself must not be, and that can only be possible through humility. Acts 20:19 says, "Serving the LORD with all humility of mind, and with many tears…" Paul said he was zealous toward God (Acts 22:3). Paul said we should be zealous of good works (Titus 2:14). Jesus said in Revelation 3:19, "Be zealous therefore, and repent." We know repentance takes humility.

The Bible mentions God's zeal for His people (Isa. 37:32). In Numbers 25:11–13, in mentioning Phinehas, it states, "He was zealous for my sake among them [Israel]….He was zealous for his God."

Having a zeal for God pleases Him, and anyone who pleased the Lord throughout the Bible had humility. We need to get passionate about the things of God and shed our mediocrity.

Jentezen Franklin said in regard to zeal and passion, "Have you ever wondered if there was one quality, one distinguishing characteristic, one accomplishment in your life that can excite God more than any other?…Well, there is, and it is not background, giftedness, or good looks. It is *passion*. God loves a person of passion. He will pass up the crowd for the person whose heart is burning with passion, zeal, desire, and holy fire. Jesus said, 'The zeal of my Father's house has eaten me up.' (See Psalm 69:9.) What is eating you up? What fires you up? Where is your desire? Where is your passion?…Passion will take you places and cause you to do things you would never do without it."

Franklin goes on to write about the passion Jesus demonstrated on the cross (Acts 1:3). He states, "When God sees passion in people, He releases His power through them." He talks about Elijah's passion and how much power he had in his life (1 Kings 17:18, 22; 18:46; 19:5, 10; 2 Kings 2:11).[2]

Zeal is something we need to have, and you can't help but be successful if you have it. Here are some of those verses that state what a humble person does:

- Fasts (1 Kings 21:27–29)
- Has a tender heart and weeps before the Lord (2 Kings 22:19)
- Prays, seeks God's face, and turns from wicked ways (2 Chron. 7:14)
- Soul boasts in the Lord (Ps. 34:2)
- Fasts and prays (Ps. 35:13)
- Has a contrite (or repentant) heart (Isa. 57:15)
- Fasts and seeks the Lord (Ezra 8:21)
- Serves the Lord (Acts 20:19)
- Is meek and longsuffering (Col. 3:12)
- Values and seeks after wisdom (Prov. 15:33)
- Is honorable (Prov. 29:23)
- Hears and increases his or her learning (Prov. 1:5)
- Willing to learn and receive instruction (Ps. 119:10, 40, 66)

Phil Pringle said, "Learning calls for humility. The proud can't learn. They can't admit ignorance and so they remain undeveloped. Humility recognizes its need for wisdom." He goes on to say, "The pursuit of wisdom is a life theme for the wise. The day we can say, 'I am now wise' does not exist. Wisdom means I do not think I am wise. She is ever my quest.... Even though we may sit under the teaching of the most brilliant communicators in the world, if we have no heart for learning they will teach us nothing. But if I have a hunger to learn, I will find lessons from the most foolish of teachers. Learning comes from hunger and humility. If we imagine we know enough, we have chosen to learn no more."[3]

> Do you see a man wise in his own eyes? There is more hope for a fool than for him.
> —PROVERBS 26:12, NKJV

Imitate Christ

R. T. Kendall points out how Jesus displayed humility in His life. He said Jesus "had to adjust to the person to whom He was talking.... He accepted people as they were. This was part of Jesus' humility. Humbling yourself, therefore, does not mean making people adjust to you; *it is making yourself adjust to them*. Satan will throw people in your path and put people around you who annoy you and get your goat.... Remember that you are praying to be more like Jesus. You have somebody in front of you that Jesus would adjust to because He humbled Himself.... Did you know that Jesus was always accountable? He was the Son of God, yet He was accountable to His Father the whole time. Paul used the little phrase in Romans 15:3, 'Even Christ did not please himself'.... He said, 'I seek to please...him who sent me' (John 5:30)."

RT goes on to say that humility leads to accomplishment. He said, "It had a final product. Paul tells us that He humbled Himself and *became obedient*.... There is a very profound reason why Jesus had to learn obedience, and it is because Jesus is the second Adam. Paul wrote: 'For just as through the disobedience of the one man the many were made sinners, so also through the obedience of the one man the many will be made righteous' (Rom.

5:19). The first Adam sinned by his disobedience. Jesus humbled Himself to become obedient, because if He were not obedient, then we would have no perfect substitute. We are, in fact, saved by His obedience."[4]

That is profound, as everything Jesus did was the fulfillment of Scripture and the perfect substitute.

Look at some of the people who received healing from Jesus. They would be people who would reflect some aspect of humility or else they wouldn't have received from Him. The Bible says in James 4:6, "God resisteth the proud, but giveth grace unto the humble." Healing is definitely receiving God's grace.

Look at the woman with the issue of blood in Matthew 9. She didn't even ask Jesus for her healing. She was so bold to say, "If I may but touch his garment, I shall be whole" (v. 21). Can you imagine not even asking? That could be seen as "too aggressive" to some. But Jesus said, "Daughter, be of good comfort; thy faith hath made thee whole" (v. 22). Anytime you are desperate for God, you must have Him first in mind, and that requires humility. She was also very bold, as she had broken the Levitical law, which stated not to go in public if you had an issue of blood (Lev. 15:19–28). There were severe consequences for her act. Ecclesiastes 8:1 states, "A man's wisdom maketh his face to shine, and the boldness of his face shall be changed." She had wisdom enough to be bold and enter the crowd to see Jesus. Boldness and confidence in Him also reflects humility.

What about blind Bartimaeus in Mark 10? It says, "He began to cry out....And many charged him that he should hold his peace: but he cried the more a great deal." And it says, "And Jesus stood still" (vv. 47–49). It got the attention of Jesus. Why did it? It was because he showed persistence. It takes humility to cry out for God's mercy in a public arena. Jesus said, "Go thy way; thy faith hath made thee whole" (v. 52). Bartimaeus received his eyesight. Persistence for the things of God is an attribute of humility.

There was the man who was let down through the roof in Mark 2. Can you imagine tearing off someone's roof? What do you think the homeowner thought? That would be considered an act that was far too aggressive. They actually committed a crime, in destroying another's property. But their reason warranted it. Jesus saw their faith, and Scripture says, "When Jesus saw their faith, he said unto the sick of the palsy, Son, thy sins be forgiven thee.... Arise, and take up thy bed" (vv. 5–9). Jesus observed desperation in them for Him and His blessings. He saw the great faith they had to go to the extreme of tearing off the roof in order to get to Him. To desperately pursue after the things of God requires humility.

Look at the woman from Canaan in Matthew 15:22–28. She desired for her daughter, who was vexed with a devil, to be delivered. Scripture says she "cried unto him, saying, Have mercy on me.... But he answered her not a word." And the disciples said to Him to send her away. Jesus said to her, "I am not sent but unto the lost sheep of the house of Israel. Then came she and worshipped him, saying, Lord, help me. But he answered and said, It is not meet to take the children's bread, and to cast it to dogs. And she said, Truth Lord: yet the dogs eat the crumbs which fall from their masters' table. Then Jesus answered and said unto her, O woman, great is thy faith: be it unto thee even as thou wilt."

Jesus was impressed with her "great" faith. Notice how Jesus first ignored her. Then she was told that He was not sent unto anyone but Israel, which she was not. She still persisted and worshiped Him, which is wisdom. He then basically said no and called her a dog. She still didn't give up but spoke her faith and determination, that she should at least get the crumbs. Some would consider her as too pushy or almost rebellious for not listening to Him. Jesus told her no twice. But Jesus obviously observed her desire to first worship Him and to not want to take no for an answer. Her persistence paid off. She also showed wisdom in her comment about the crumbs. That was an impressive comeback! She showed wisdom in coming to Him and humility by worshiping Him.

One more person to observe: the centurion in Matthew 8:5–10. He desired his servant to be healed. Jesus said He would come and heal him. The centurion said, "Lord, I am not worthy that thou shouldest come under my roof: but speak the word only, and my servant shall be healed." He understood authority, and it was not necessary that Jesus even come, as he also was a man under authority. If Jesus simply spoke the word only, it would be sufficient. Scripture says, "When Jesus heard it, he marvelled, and said to them that followed, Verily I say unto you, I have not found so great faith, no, not in Israel." Jesus marveled at the centurion's understanding of His authority. So obviously, being a person submitted to authority, especially the authority of God, is also an attribute of humility.

In 1 Peter 5:1–6, Peter tells us to not to be "lords over God's heritage [God's people], but being examples to the flock. . . . be subject one to another, and be clothed with humility." To not lord over someone reflects humility, as the opposite would be pride.

There are many examples in the Bible where humility brought actual riches, as our verse in Proverbs 22:4 mentions.

In 2 Chronicles 32:25–27 it states, "Hezekiah didn't respond with true thanksgiving and praise for he had become proud. . . . But finally Hezekiah and the residents of Jerusalem humbled themselves....So Hezekiah became very wealthy and was highly honored" (TLB). The wealth came after the humility.

So to summarize, the characteristics of a humble person are: a contrite spirit, a teachable heart, a determination for the things of God, zeal and passion, obedience, submissiveness to authority (especially God's), and an uncompromised and loving attitude. Obedience to His Word encapsulates most all of these individual characteristics.

One more point in regard to obedience: if we obey Him, which shows we are humble, Jesus said in John 15:14, "You are my friends, if ye do whatsoever I command you." That is quite a statement. God only called two in the Old Testament His friends: Moses (Exod. 33:11) and Abraham (2 Chron. 20:7; Isa. 41:8; James 2:23). How blessed we are to be called His friends.

One of the most humble people on the earth, according to most who know him, is Billy Graham. Allen Emery, who served on Billy's board for decades, was sharing about a time after one of Billy's first crusades, when he was speaking at a Sunday school to a group of New England pastors. He said that after speaking, "There was quite a response, much more than expected! That was my first association with Billy, and his profound humility came through and a sense of purpose, a sense of direction....He wanted us to pray with him. He said, 'The one thing I want you to pray for is this: That I will not take credit for the successes of these things whatsoever, because if I do, my lips will turn to clay.' He never did take any credit. He never let anybody make him a big shot. It's humility I have never seen in anybody else....But in Billy they saw someone completely up front about everything; a man without guile."[5]

Dr. Billy Graham is a truly exceptional person. Most have

commented they have never met anyone with more integrity, more humility, and yet of such a commanding presence than he.

Humility Prevails

I was interviewed by a corporation that owned twenty-six condominiums in a certain complex. They were interviewing several companies to market these properties. I was the third interview. Now at this time, my company was down to just me. It was just after the drop in the early 1990s, and the market was quite depressed.

After hearing what the president of that corporation told me about the other companies, I knew I was not in their league, as they were mega offices, had a large staff, and big advertising budget. I had only one assistant and a small budget. I explained to him that I had been in the business for twenty years and was very familiar with the area and that particular tract. I had sold several units there before. I told him, however, I was not able to compete with the other offices he interviewed, and he would be better off with one of the others. To my surprise, he said, "No, I'm going to choose you. Since you were honest with me about your inferior position, I know you will tell me the truth about the values of our properties and also will not misrepresent us by lying or exaggerating to the buyers. We want someone we can trust. We can always help with the money for advertizing. Ads you can buy; integrity you cannot."

Telling the truth has always caused me to prosper. Many wish to exaggerate and puff themselves up, not realizing that "pride goeth before destruction, and an haughty spirit before a fall" (Prov. 16:18). Remember the story Jesus told about the man being invited to a wedding (Luke 14:8–11). He said to take the lower seat in the house. In doing that, when the one in charge sees you in a lower place, he will be able to honor you by bringing you higher.

By the way, I ended up selling all twenty-six condominiums and even listed some others as a result. Proverbs 22:4 states, "By humility and the fear of the LORD are riches, and honour and life."

What Are You Willing to Do for a Friend?

I worked at a large real estate office for quite some time, and there was one friend named Glen that I used to talk to daily. He was a very successful agent, very likable person, and he was not a Christian. I would share some biblical things with him on occasion, but he was not interested in the subject at all. He felt it was fine for me but not for him. I knew it bothered him to talk about it, so I didn't bring it up any more. We got along well, as we had the business in common. I felt that God had so much He wanted to do with him.

Well, one day I was praying for him, and the Lord impressed me to fast. I decided to do a seven-day water fast. Now I don't like fasting but especially nothing at all. After the fast, on the eighth morning, I came into the office as usual. A little later on that day, Glen arrived and had a very startled look on his face. I said, "Glen, are you all right?" He said, "Bill, I have got to tell you what happened to me last night." I said, "Please, go ahead."

Starting off rather slowly and obviously a bit shaken, he said, "I came home last night and pulled into my garage, turned off the car, and suddenly, this bright light appeared in my garage. I got out of the car and immediately fell on my knees. The bright light was Jesus. I didn't see His face but just this bright light. I knew who it was. There is no mistaking Him. He said to me, 'Why do you deny Me? Why do you fight against Me?' I just began weeping, and I asked Him to forgive me. I asked Him into my life. Bill, I am now a Christian. Can you believe that?" I said, "Yes, I can, as I have always felt that you were called to serve Him, even though you were not interested in the least."

It is interesting that Jesus appeared to him at the very end of my fast. I never told him I prayed and fasted for him. Then, a few years after that, he and his wife moved away to another state, and I never saw or heard from him again. Then, just last year, which was twenty-five years later, I received a call from him. He saw my book in a store and called me. Well, he told me he had been very involved in his church as a leader, held Bible studies, and had been serving God ever since. I finally told him the story about my fasting, and he was shocked. He said to me, "Why didn't you ever tell me? I can't believe I was unaware of this all these years. What if you hadn't done that for me? Thank you so very much. I have had a wonderful life because of knowing Jesus." Thank the Lord for His goodness!

After that occurrence all those years ago, I decided to do more fasting for others. I have seen many give their hearts to the Lord since. Fasting is a principle in the Bible that really does work. If you have a family member who is stubborn, then I encourage you to fast. The time period is not important. Whatever you feel led to do, then just do it. Fasting also reflects humility, as Psalm 35:13 states, "I humbled my soul with fasting; and my prayer." Psalm 49:8 says, "For the redemption of their soul is precious."

The Small Matters Matter!

I was a personal friend of the pastor of a church I attended for a long time. His staff always asked me to sit up front with the pastor, but I always declined. I did this for several reasons. First, I didn't want it to appear that I was getting special treatment because of our friendship. I didn't want anyone to have any reason to say, "Look at him; he thinks he is a big shot being escorted up to the front." It's not that I really was worried about what they thought of me, but rather, that they might look at it as church politics and favoritism. I didn't want the pastor to look bad either by giving me special treatment. Besides, I never liked attention drawn to myself anyway. I always sat in the back of the room. I would never give a speech at school, as I disliked public speaking to the point where I would get sick over it. That is another reason I did not want to share my experience with the world in my book *23 Minutes in Hell*. The publisher came to us and asked us to write the book. We never would self-promote it in any way and still haven't to this day. My point is I am simply trying to show that even a simple thing such as where we would sit can help develop humility in us. Or, if we succumb to the special treatment, we could become prideful. Little things in life can help shape our attitudes and form certain characteristics. My wife and I have learned that humility is definitely the most attractive attribute in a person. God will truly lift us up, if we will first lower ourselves (Luke 14:8–11).

CHAPTER 17

THE FEAR OF GOD

IN THE PREVIOUS chapter, we looked at the first part of Proverbs 22:4 dealing with humility. Now let's look at the second part on fearing God.

There are two sides to this fear. First of all, if you are a Christian, God is your loving Father and desires for you to come to Him boldly and in confidence. (See John 1:12; 8:44; 17:9; Romans 9:7–8; Galatians 3:26; Ephesians 5:1; 2 Thessalonians 3:4; Hebrews 4:16; 10:35; 1 John 2:28.) His desire is for us to feel completely at peace communing with Him in our everyday lives. We are told to call Him Abba (Daddy) Father (Rom. 8:15). Just as we can understand a loving father's relationship with us, we are to view our relationship with Him and much more so.

I know there are many who have a distorted view of a father and son or daughter relationship, as some fathers have not displayed the love of God in any manner. However, this is not how our heavenly Father is in any way. Our heavenly Father gave the most precious person He has, His only Son, for us. His love for us far exceeds our love (Eph. 3:19).

The other side to this fear is for us to have a reverential awe and an actual shaking in terror of an almighty and infinitely powerful holy God. Psalm 89:7 states, "God is greatly to be feared in the assembly of the saints." The word *feared* is the Hebrew word *aras*. In *Strong's*, it means "to shake in terror." Hebrews 12:21 states, "Moses said, I exceedingly fear and quake" in God's presence. And Moses was called the friend of God. So how much more should we (Acts 5:11; 9:31; Rom. 11:20)?

The first reason I want to point out as to why we are to fear God is *because Jesus did*. In Hebrews 5:7 it says, "Who in the days of his flesh, when he had offered up prayers and supplications with strong crying and tears unto him that was able to save him from death, and was heard in that he *feared*; though he were a Son, yet learned he obedience by the things which he suffered" (emphasis added). That one reason is good enough for me. Yet there are many reasons why we are to fear Him. Jesus is our example, and if even the Son of God can fear His Father, then how much more you and I.

The only way we can get to know someone is to spend time with them. And the only way we can fall in love with them is to have spent time together. The Bible says to "taste and see that the LORD is good" (Ps. 34:8).

John Bevere says, "You can only love someone to the extent that you know them.... Our love for God is limited by a lack of holy fear."[1] As we develop a reverential fear of God, we can't help but fall in love with Him. Jesus prayed to the Father in John 17:26 "that the love wherewith thou hast loved me may be in them, and I in them."

Another reason we are to fear God is because He is holy. Peter also said, "But as he which hath called you is holy, so be ye holy in all manner of conversation; because it is written, Be ye holy, for I am holy. And if ye call on the Father, who without respect of persons judgeth according to every man's work, pass the time of your sojourning here in *fear*" (1 Pet. 1:15–17, emphasis added). (See also Ephesians 1:4; 1 Thessalonians 4:7; Hebrews 12:14.) Romans 7:13 states that "sin by the commandment might become exceeding sinful." In other words, sin should become to us as God sees it: "exceeding sinful." He hates sin, and He is too pure to even look upon it (Hab. 1:13). Psalm 119:140 says, "Thy word is very pure." For us to live in sin shows such disrespect to God. We have been made dead to sin (Rom. 6:10–14; 1 Pet. 4:1), but we must renew our minds with His Word (Rom. 12:2).

Our goal should not be simply to resist sin, but we should actually come to the point where we hate sin and won't even be tempted to give in to it. Psalm 97:10 says, "Ye that love the LORD hate evil." We should be able to say, "I hate vain thoughts....I hate every false way....I hate and abhor lying" (Ps. 119:113, 128, 163). Romans 6:12 says, "Therefore do not let sin reign in your mortal body, that you should obey it in its lusts" (NKJV).

We are not to be halfhearted or half-committed. If we serve Him with all our heart, we will obey His Word and avoid sin. Psalm 119:34 says, "Give me understanding, and I shall keep thy law; yea, I shall observe it with my *whole* heart" (emphasis added).

David said again in Psalm 119:11, "Thy word have I hid in mine heart, that I might not sin against thee."

His grace empowers us to be able to walk free of sin: "Let us have grace, whereby we may serve God acceptably with reverence and godly fear" (Heb. 12:28).

Sometimes we may tend to view God like we would see ourselves. We might think, "Well, sin is really not that big a deal." However, it is a big deal to God. My brother, Pastor Patrick Wiese, in a teaching on Jeremiah 9:23–24 called "Understanding God and His Ways," explains God's process and how we can understand His perspective on justice and judgment. He explains thoroughly this powerful point and teaching on his website. It is worth your read. This is only an excerpt, but even this much explains it in a way I had never heard.

> God is 100% just (righteous), not 50% just and 50% mercy. He doesn't say, "I am in a good mood today, so I will overlook their sin." No, He is 100% just all the time, so sin must always be punished. Unlike man, God will not compromise. Man is worthy of 100% of God's wrath and judgment on sin. However, since God is also 100% love, He did not leave man in his hopeless state. In order to satisfy God's wrath on sin, He poured out the full punishment on Jesus on the cross, meeting His requirement of complete justice. He showed 100 % justice by the cruel crucifixion, and He also showed 100% love in that He gave His only Son in our place.[2]

For further study, read: Numbers 14:18; Isaiah 13:11; 53:1–5; Romans 1:18; 5:8, 15–19; 1 Corinthians 15:3–4; 2 Corinthians 5:21; Galatians 3:22; 2 Peter 2:9; 1 John 4:16.

Wayne Grudem said, "But when Christ's sufferings at last came to an end on the cross, it showed that he had borne the full measure of God's wrath against sin and there was no penalty left to pay."[3]

This next explanation will hopefully give a clearer understanding as to why our sin is so offensive to God. We need to understand that because we are sinning against a holy and infinitely powerful Supreme Being, it is deserving of eternal punishment.

Thomas Aquinas said, "Now a sin that is against God is infinite; the higher the person against whom it is committed, the graver the sin. It is more criminal to strike a head of state than a private citizen—and God is of infinite greatness. Therefore an infinite punishment is deserved for a sin committed against him."[4]

To further explain, Christopher W. Morgan states, "If an angry teenage boy punched his mother, he would deserve more punishment than if he punched his older brother. The relationship and the offended party do matter. It is also important to remember that God is not only different from human beings in degree; he is also different in being. If in a robbery, the gunman shoots and kills the owner of the house, he should receive a greater punishment than if he killed the family cat (as much as this writer loves cats!). Thus, because sin is against God, and God is infinitely worthy of obedience, sin merits an infinite punishment."[5]

So the greater the one sinned against, the graver the sin.

Also, God sent His most precious Son to die for us. Many people reject what God values most. They are, in essence, saying to God, "I do not value what You value. Your Son means nothing to me; so don't bother me with Your views. I have my own." As a matter of fact, people even use His Son's name as a curse word throughout their entire lives. How would you feel if you gave up your own son to die for someone and they blasphemed his name and even denied that he existed?

Hebrews 10:29 states, "Of how much worse punishment, do you suppose, will he be thought worthy who has trampled the Son of God underfoot, counted the blood of the covenant by which he was sanctified a common thing, and insulted the Spirit of grace?" (NKJV). Those in the New Testament are worthy of a greater punishment than those in the Old Testament (v. 28) because they did not value the blood of God's Son shed for them. They considered Him nothing special but a common thing. It goes on to say, "It is a fearful thing to fall into the hands of the living God" (v. 31, NKJV).

God hates all sin, but there are also varying degrees of sin. Jesus said to Pilate in John 19:11, "He that delivered me unto thee hath the greater sin." In Matthew 23:14, Jesus mentions that the hypocrites "shall receive the greater damnation." In Proverbs 6:16–17 the Lord lists six things He hates, "yea, seven are an abomination unto him."

Yet, even though God hates sin, He is a God of great mercy and grace (Ps. 86:5; 145:8–9). He gives many warnings and time for us to change our ways. He shows man His goodness, His patience, His kindness, and His forgiveness. Psalm 86:5 states, "For thou, Lord, art good, and ready to forgive, and plenteous in mercy unto all them that call upon thee." (See also Psalm 145:8–9; Luke 6:35; Romans 15:5; Revelation 1:9.) His desire is to see everyone repent and receive Him as their Lord and Savior and enter heaven (John 5:40; 6:40; 11:25–26; Acts 2:21; Rom. 10:13; Eph. 2:8–9; 1 Tim. 2:4–6; 2 Pet. 3:9). He will never force anyone to believe in Him. Actually, the only time Jesus ever used force was when He threw people *out* of the temple (Matt. 21:12; Mark 11:15; Luke 19:45; John 2:14–15). He never forced anyone in!

The main reason why God hates sin is because it separates us from Him, and His desire is to have a relationship with us and bless us. He is able to bless us through our obedience to His Word (Josh. 1:8; Job 36:11; Ps. 37:4; Isa. 1:19; Luke 12:32).

Some of the church simply think, "Well, I am 'under grace,' and God really doesn't mind my sin. He will overlook my short-comings, since He is a loving God."

No, He won't overlook our sins (Exod. 34:7; Num. 14:18; Prov. 24:12; Matt. 16:27; Rev. 20:13–14). Romans 8:13 says, "For if ye live after the flesh, ye shall die." Jesus said in Mark 9:47, "And if thine eye offend thee, pluck it out: it is better for thee to enter into the kingdom of God with one eye, than having two eyes to be cast into hell fire." The word *offend* in *Strong's* means "cause to sin, to fall away." In other words, if you are living a lifestyle of habitual sin, you will end up in hell (1 Cor. 6:9–10; Gal. 5:19–21; Eph. 5:5; Rev. 21:8). Hebrews 10:26–27 states, "For if we sin willfully after that we have received the knowledge of the truth, there remaineth no more sacrifice for sins, but a certain fearful looking for of judgment and fiery indignation, which shall devour the adversaries." If we do sin, and repent, He will forgive us (1 John 1:9).

We hear of many Christian leaders falling into sin. Some have indicated that their problem wasn't that they didn't love God, but that they didn't fear Him. Proverbs 16:6 states, "By the fear of the LORD men depart from evil." Jeremiah 32:40 says, "I will put my fear in their hearts, that they shall not depart from me."

We are called to walk in holiness, and you don't see much of that today. Hebrews 12:14 says, "Follow peace with all men, and holiness, without which no man shall see the Lord." (See also 1 Thessalonians 4:7.)

R. T. Kendall again states, "A deep and true fear of God

will keep you from committing adultery because of what it does to God, the Church, the one you would be involved with, your spouse, family, and you....We do not act in a manner we know would bring Him displeasure....A healthy Christian fears God's chastening and discipline." RT goes on to say, "The fear of God is a no-nonsense and no-joke reality. It is very real when described in the Bible and is often intended to strike fear in us....It certainly does mean to worship with reverence and awe, but it also means to live in fear of displeasing the Lord."[6]

It is God's grace that empowers us to be able to live a lifestyle that abstains from sin.

John Bevere states, "Grace has been taught as simply God's unmerited favor. It is indeed His favor and cannot be bought or earned. However, it also empowers us to obey, and the evidence that we've truly received it is our godly lifestyle. Our obedience to His Word confirms grace's reality in our lives."[7]

John also says, "Grace enables and empowers us to live a life of holiness and obedience to the authority of God."[8]

As for obedience, Keith A. Butler states, "If you are a parent and you tell your child to clean his room, when do you expect him to do it? When he feels like it?...No, you expect him to do it when you tell him to do it. You might go to his room two hours after you told him to clean it up and find that no one's been there. So you yell out, 'Didn't I tell you to clean your room?' And he might answer, 'I'm coming!' Then five minutes later he still hasn't shown up and has a number of excuses....As a parent, your reaction to this kind of behavior is not one of pleasure. When your child behaves like that, you are not inclined to bless him....Well, then, what in the world makes Christians think that it's okay for them to obey God when they get ready to? They wait until they feel like obeying Him and then expect all His blessings to just fall on them. It doesn't work that way."[9]

David said in Psalm 119:63, "I am a companion of all them that fear thee, and of them that keep thy precepts." Notice the association of fearing Him and keeping His precepts. The two go together. If we fear Him, we will desire to keep His Word in our hearts (Ps. 119:11).

When Ananias lied to the Holy Ghost (Acts 5:1–5) and didn't repent, he dropped dead. The Bible says, "Great fear came on all them that heard these things" (vv. 7–11). And this is the New Testament! What caused Ananias to lie? Well, he wouldn't have lied if he had feared God. After that took place, I'm sure others in the church and town must have been thinking, "I thought I knew God, but I must not!" They would have remembered Jesus as being sweet and loving, and He was. But now, seeing the severity of one dropping dead in church from lying? They would have been examining themselves with the thought, "That could have been me." In the Book of Proverbs, it says, "The fear of the Lord is to hate evil" (Prov. 8:13). Psalm 97:10 says, "Ye that love the Lord, hate evil." The church congregation must have considered verses as such and realized that they may not have been hating evil either. Would they be the next one to drop dead?

A No-Fear Culture

We live in a culture where most do not fear God at all. Much of our current society has little or no respect for authority. This dishonoring of authority has led to an absence of the fear of the Lord, even in the church.

R. T. Kendall said, "We live in what Dr. O. S. Hawkins calls the 'no-fear culture.' OS suggests it is because 'our generation knows little of the nature of God.' He defines the fear of God as being 'a reverential awe; a sense of being afraid of offending a holy God in any way.'"[10]

Today, our society does not even call a sin a sin. We have "issues," but please don't call it that archaic "sin" word. Others mock sin (Prov. 14:9) or laugh at the mention of it (Prov. 15:21).

John Bunyan said, "Fools make a mock at sin, will not believe, it has a fearful dagger up its sleeve; How can it be, they say, that such a thing so full of sweetness, e'er should wear a sting. They know not that it is the very spell of sin, to make them laugh themselves to hell. Look to thyself then, deal with sin no more. Lest He who saves, against thee shuts the door."[11]

In today's culture, tolerance has become the high moral ground instead of truth. It has become socially and politically incorrect to not accept any and all beliefs, no matter how vile or perverted. If one stands for righteousness, he is labeled as an extremist or prejudiced. You don't even have to come against anyone at all, just simply stand for good and you're considered myopic and narrow-minded, and even hateful.

Isaiah 5:20 states, "Woe unto them that call evil good, and good evil." Proverbs 21:10 says, "The soul of the wicked desireth evil." Psalm 94:20 mentions rulers who practice iniquity, "which frameth mischief by a law." They make a law in order to carry out their evil agenda. This is where many of our leaders are right now. But God says in Psalm 38:20, "They also that render evil for good are mine adversaries." You don't want to be God's adversary!

Many do not realize that God instructs us to obey His law in order to be protected and blessed, personally and as a nation. Psalm 33:12 states, "Blessed is the nation whose God is the LORD." And Proverbs 14:34 says, "Righteousness exalteth a nation." His law is not to restrict us but to benefit us. God warns us of sin and its affects.

Billy Graham said, "The Ten Commandments tell us not to covet or lust. However, all moral law is more than a test; it is for our own good. Every law which God has given is for our benefit. If a person breaks it, he is not only rebelling against God, he is hurting himself. God gave 'the law' because he loves man. It is for man's benefit. God's commandments were given to protect and promote man's happiness, not to restrict it."[12]

A. W. Tozer said, "Men and women reject this message for the same reason they have rejected all of the Bible. They do not wish to be under the authority of the moral Word of God."[13]

Charles Colson states, "Christianity gives an absolute moral law that allows us to judge between right and wrong.... Without moral absolutes, there is no real basis for ethics. An absolute moral law doesn't confine people in a straitjacket of Victorian prudery. People will always debate the boundaries of moral law and its varied applications. But the very idea of right and wrong makes sense only if there is a final standard, a measuring rod, by which we can make moral judgments."[14]

Much of the world actually has an entitlement attitude, even in regard to heaven. Many believe they are pretty decent folk and expect to enter through the pearly gates. They don't want to be held accountable for their actions, yet still feel justified in stating they are "good people." Even by their own mediocre standards, they would not measure up. Man only need show some humility and repent (Luke 13:3; Acts 17:30–31), and God would forgive him. In James 4:6 it states, "God resisteth the proud, but giveth grace unto the humble." Again, Jesus told us, "Go and sin no more." (See John 5:14; 8:11.) A wise person would fear Him and obey Him, as there is a wrath coming on sin (Rom. 1:18; 2 Pet. 2:9). The good news is we can escape the wrath by repenting (Acts 26:20; 1 Thess. 1:9–10).

In C. S. Lewis's book *The Lion, the Witch, and the Wardrobe*, we read these unforgettable lines:

> "Ooh," said Susan, "…is he—quite safe? I shall feel rather nervous about meeting a lion."
>
> "That you will, dearie, and no mistake," said Mrs. Beaver; "if there is anyone who can appear before Aslan without their knees knocking, they're either braver than most or else just silly."
>
> "Then he isn't safe?" said Lucy.
>
> "Safe?" said Mr. Beaver; "don't you hear what Mrs. Beaver tells you? Who said anything about safe? 'Course he isn't safe. But he's good. He's the King, I tell you."[15]

Martin Luther said, "You must know God as your enemy before you can know Him as your friend."[16]

Learning to Fear God

So how do we attain this healthy fear of Almighty God? Proverbs 1:29 states, "They hated knowledge, and did not choose the fear of the Lord." God always gives us a choice, and lets us know the consequences. David said, "I have chosen the way of truth: thy judgments have I laid before me.…I have chosen thy precepts" (Ps. 119:30, 173).

Here is how we attain this fear: we must "incline thine ear unto wisdom, and apply thine heart to understanding; yea, if thou criest after knowledge, and liftest up thy voice for understanding; if thou seekest her as silver, and searchest for her as for hid treasures; *then shalt thou understand the fear of the Lord*, and find the knowledge of God" (Prov. 2:2–5, emphasis added). You see, we have to go after God wholeheartedly. (See Psalm 111:1; 119:2, 10, 34, 58, 69, 145.) Once we come to understand that He expects obedience and hates sin, we begin developing a healthy, reverential fear of Him.

Here are some verses that state just what the fear of the Lord is and how to obtain it:

- Tithe to learn the fear of the Lord (Deut. 14:23).

- Read and study God's Word all the days of your life to learn to fear the Lord (Deut. 17:19).

- Be taught the fear of the Lord (Ps. 34:11).

- Change your ways in order to show that you fear God (Ps. 55:19).

- His Word must be established in you if you fear Him (Ps. 119:38).

- Trembling flesh shows you fear the Lord (Ps. 119:120).

- The fear of the Lord is the beginning of knowledge (Prov. 1:7).

- The fear of the Lord is to hate evil (Prov. 8:13).

- The fear of the Lord is the beginning of wisdom (Prov. 9:10).

- The fear of the Lord is to depart from evil (Prov. 16:6).

Here are some verses that state the benefits to those who fear the Lord:

- He will honor you (Ps. 15:4).

- He will tell you His secrets (Ps. 25:14).

- He will lay up His goodness for you (Ps. 31:19).

- His eye will be on you (Ps. 33:18).

- The angel of the Lord will encamp around you (Ps. 34:7).

- You will not lack anything (Ps. 34:9).

- His salvation will be near you (Ps. 85:9).

- The Lord will pity you (Ps. 103:13).

- He will give you meat (Ps. 111:5).

- The Lord will be your help and shield (Ps. 115:11).

- He will fulfill your desires (Ps. 145:19).

- The Lord will take pleasure in you (Ps. 147:11).

- You will have wisdom, and your days will be multiplied (Prov. 9:10–11).

- Your days will be prolonged (Prov. 10:27).

- You will have strong confidence and a place of refuge (Prov. 14:26).

- You will be satisfied and evil will not visit you (Prov. 19:23).

- You will have riches, honor, and life (Prov. 22:4).

- It will be well with you (Eccles. 8:12).

As you can see, the fear of the Lord is of great benefit to those who have it. Look at just that one verse in Proverbs 19: "He shall not be visited with evil" (v. 23). That is an awesome promise.

No evil will come near you (Prov. 12:21). All of us would want that, right? The bottom line is to have the fear of the Lord, which causes us to remain close to Him and keeps us from evil (Prov. 16:6; Jer. 32:40).

So how do we reconcile being able to come to Him as a warm and loving Father, yet still maintain a reverential and godly fear?

When I was growing up, I feared my dad if I did something wrong. I would get a spanking or punished in some way. But that didn't mean I would never feel comfortable with him again. No, I respected his authority. But I knew he loved me and would never hurt me. In the same way, we are to fear God, but, in addition, have an awe and respect of an almighty and holy God who will execute judgment and justice (Jer. 23:5).

Micah 5:15 says, "And I will execute vengeance in anger and fury upon the heathen, such as they have not heard." In Isaiah 13:11, 13, God says, "And I will punish the world for their evil.... Therefore I will shake the heavens, and the earth shall remove out of her place, in the wrath of the LORD of hosts, and in the day of his fierce anger."

That doesn't sound good! Our God is a loving God, but He is also a righteous judge (Deut. 32:4; Ps. 96:13; Acts 17:31). Our desire should be one of not wanting to displease Him or hurt Him by sinning against Him.

There are times when it is appropriate to come to God as "Daddy" Father and other times not. There are times when He chooses to manifest Himself in His holy presence. In those times, we are to show careful reverence and stand in fear and trembling. In Ezekiel 38:20 it states, "All the men that are on the face of the earth, shall shake at my presence." Jeremiah 23:9 says, "All my bones shake...because of the LORD, and because of the words of his holiness." In 2 Corinthians 5:11 Paul said, "Knowing therefore the terror of the Lord, we persuade men." He understood the terror of a holy God at the judgment seat where "every one may receive the things done in his body, according to that he hath done, whether it be good or bad" (v. 10). Then it is recorded in Hebrews 12:21, "Moses said, I exceedingly fear and quake."

There were many times the Israelites did not reverence Him with a holy fear, but they were *afraid* of Him. There is a difference in fearing Him and being afraid of Him. They were afraid of Him because they did not keep His commandments. In Deuteronomy 5:29, God said, "O that there were such an heart in them, that they would fear me, and keep my commandments always that it might be well with them, and with their children for ever!" God's heart is that we would fear Him in order for it to be well with us.

This next verse in Exodus points out the difference in the two fears. Exodus 20:18–21 states, "And all the people saw the thunderings.... And they said unto Moses, Speak thou with us, and we will hear: but let not God speak with us, lest we die. And Moses said unto the people, *Fear not*: for God is come to prove you, and that his *fear may be* before your faces, that ye sin not" (emphasis added).

Two things to notice: First, it says that they were afraid of God, but Moses told them *not to* be afraid. However, in the same verse, Moses said that God desires that "his *fear may be* before their faces." Obviously, there are two different types of fear Moses is mentioning here. Second, they need not be afraid of their God and should have been anxious to hear from Him. Yet at the same time, they also needed to show a reverence and godly fear of Him, which is a different kind of fear.

The godly fear comes only by obeying His commandments.

Obedience would demonstrate that they feared Him in a reverential way. However, they didn't show a reverential and holy fear, because of their sinful lifestyle. They only wanted to hear Moses, because they knew they were not right with God and His holy presence would expose their sin. In John 3:20–21 Jesus said, "For every one that doeth evil hateth the light, neither cometh to the light, lest, his deeds should be reproved. But he that doeth truth cometh to the light." If they would have been obeying God, they would have reverenced Him and desired to come to Him. But they were instead afraid of Him. God knew their hearts were not right.

In 2 Chronicles 6:26–31 it states, "When the heaven is shut up, and there is no rain, because they have sinned against thee; yet if they pray toward this place, and confess thy name, and turn from their sin, when thou dost afflict them…and render unto every man according unto all his ways…that they may fear thee, to walk in his ways."

God needed to shut up the heavens because of their sin, yet He would forgive them if they prayed. He let them know that they would be judged for their ways, which would place the fear of God in their hearts. Verse 24 says, "And if thy people Israel be put to the worst before the enemy, because they have sinned against thee…" This also shows that because of disobedience, the enemy would triumph over them until they prayed and made supplications before God. They needed to learn the hard way.

The point also in explaining all of this is there is a difference in being afraid of God and in fearing Him. You may be afraid of an enemy, but you don't fear him in a reverential way.

If you have ever driven a very fast car, you have a respect for the power. Now, not to compare God to a car, but my point is, you can understand the respect for a powerful automobile. If you don't handle it right, it can kill you. You respect its power. It is the same with God, as we should respect His awesome power and His judgment on sin.

Again, in Deuteronomy 5:29, do you see God's heart here? His desire was that it would be well with them and their children. He was concerned for them as a loving Father and wanted so much for them to stay close to Him. That is always God's heart toward His people. God is not standing there with a big hammer and just waiting for us to cross the line. No, He is watching for an opportunity to bless us, not punish us. His discipline is gentle, and He warns us over and over before more severe measures are needed. He never will hurt us. If we continue to ignore all His warnings, He then would have to draw back from us. We walk out from under His protection. Then the enemy can get through to hurt us. There is also a curse over all the earth because of fallen man and sin (Lev. 18:25; Isa. 24:5; 33:9; Zech. 5:3). The curse is operating all the time. Just as when rain falls, we will get wet unless we stay under the umbrella. God's hand keeps us protected, as He is that umbrella. If He removes His hand of protection from us, it is because of our continual disobedience, and we can be attacked by the wicked one. We are the ones who first walk out from under the umbrella (Deut. 11:26–28; 30:5–20).

Here are some examples of how God had to withdraw His hand of protection, yet He pleaded with them to come back to Him:

- Deuteronomy 31:17—"Then mine anger shall be kindled against them in that day, and I will forsake them, and I will hide my face from them, and they shall be devoured, and many evils and troubles shall befall them; so that they will say in that day, Are not these evils come upon us, *because our God is not among us*?" (emphasis added).

- Jeremiah 3:12–13—"'*Come home to me again*, for I am merciful....Only acknowledge your guilt. Admit that you rebelled against the LORD your God'" (NLT, emphasis added).

- Jeremiah 5:1—"'Run up and down every street...,' says the LORD. 'Look high and low; search throughout the city! If you can find even one just and honest person, I will not destroy the city'" (NLT).

- Jeremiah 8:4–5—"When they discover they're on the wrong road, don't they turn back? Then why do these people stay on their self-destructive path? Why do the people...refuse to turn back [even though I warned them]?" (NLT).

- Jeremiah 25:4–9—"And the LORD hath sent unto you all his servants the prophets...but ye have not hearkened....They said, Turn ye again every one from his evil way...and dwell in the land that the LORD hath given unto you....Yet ye have not hearkened unto me, saith the LORD; that ye might provoke me to anger with the works of your hands *to your own hurt*" (emphasis added).

- Jeremiah 26:3—"Perhaps they will listen and turn from their evil ways. Then I will change my mind about the disaster I am ready to pour out on them because of their sins" (NLT).

- Jeremiah 44:4–5—"Again and again I sent my servants, the prophets, to plead with them, 'Don't do these horrible things that I hate so much.' But my people would not listen or turn back from their wicked ways" (NLT).

- Lamentations 3:33 (NLT)—"For he [God] does not enjoy hurting people or causing them sorrow." The Lord has no pleasure in allowing punishment. The Lord over and over pleads for people to simply turn back to Him for He delights in showing mercy.

- Romans 2:4—"Don't you see how wonderfully kind, tolerant, and patient God is with you? Does this mean nothing to you? Can't you see that his kindness is intended to turn you from your sin?" (NLT)

You can see God's heart here! He clearly let them know how to avoid the evil, but they simply refused His instruction and goodness. They did not fear Him in the right way, but in the last days Hosea 3:5 says that Israel "shall fear the Lord and his goodness." The *New Spirit-Filled Life Bible* points out that *fear*, or *pachad* (pah-chad) in Hebrew, means "to be startled, to tremble, to stand in awe, to revere, or fear; be amazed." *Pachad* concerns a person's reaction to something sudden and startling to the point of trembling. The verb appears twenty-four times. The noun (*pachad*), which refers to something dreadful and awe-producing, occurs more than forty times.[17] Here Israel will tremble because of God's startling, sudden, amazing goodness showered upon them in the latter days! This verse shows how positive the Hebrew concept for fear, trembling, and reverence can be, as does Proverbs 28:14: "Happy is the man who is always reverent [*pachad*]" (NKJV).

I don't know how or why God puts up with mankind, but I'm glad He does. His patience is astounding. May we learn through

His Word and not have to learn the hard way. The more we grow from glory to glory, the more we fall in love with Him, and the more we hate sin. In the earlier stages of our walk, we resist sin. But as we grow, we no longer struggle to resist sin because we hate it. We lose all desire for anything ungodly.

> Ye that love the LORD, hate evil.
>
> —PSALM 97:10

> O how love I thy law!
>
> —PSALM 119:97

> I hate every false way.
>
> —PSALM 119:104

> I hate vain thoughts.
>
> —PSALM 119:113

> The fear of the LORD is to hate evil.
>
> —PROVERBS 8:13

This will be our attitude once we have matured in Him. And the way we do this is simple: hide His Word in our hearts (Ps. 119:11). That is one of the wisest things a man could do!

CHAPTER 18

LIFE AND DEATH ARE WITHIN YOUR POWER

O UR OWN MOUTH is what gets us in trouble. If we could learn to bridle our tongue, we could control our lives. Our words are not only important but also crucial. We can speak blessing or cursing. Proverbs 18:21 says, "Death and life are in the power of the tongue." That is a powerful statement. This New Testament verse makes it even clearer:

> Behold also the ships, which though they be so great, and are driven of fierce winds, yet are they turned about with a very small helm, whithersoever the governor listeth. Even so the tongue is a little member, and boasteth great things. Behold how great a matter

a little fire kindleth! And the tongue is a fire, a world of iniquity: so is the tongue among our members, that it defileth the whole body, and setteth on fire the course of nature; and it is set on fire of hell.... But the tongue can no man tame.... Out of the same mouth proceedeth blessings and cursing. My brethren, these things ought not so to be.

—JAMES 3:4–10

James tells us that the tongue steers our whole life, just as the helm turns a great ship. It is a small member, but it can accomplish much. He tells us that no man can tame it. It is interesting to note that man has learned how to control even some things in nature. He can make a horse obey by a small bit in his mouth. He can control a ship in the great oceans with a small rudder. He can even tame a lion. But a small member of our flesh, the tongue, we cannot tame. We have to control our tongues ourselves, just as we do lust. It is part of our flesh that God will not control for us.

R. T. Kendall states in his book *Controlling the Tongue*, "James elaborates on the danger of the uncontrolled tongue in these lines (James 3:3–8).... Conversion did not conquer the tongue problem.... What is James's point if there is nothing we can do and there is nothing God promises to do?... It is a wake-up call to take responsibility for our words and deeds so that we will be consciously aware and able to improve. God made us in such a way that we do change by being warned and seeing the consequences. We do! We are more likely to change when we see the danger and results if we don't change.... Some may wish to say, 'Man can't tame the tongue, but God can.' Yes, He can indeed. But He probably won't. God can do a lot of things. He can stop hurricanes. He can stop earthquakes. He can stop crime. I used to say at Westminster Chapel, 'Boys and girls, God can do your homework for you.' But He never did mine! God motivates us by a strong word of warning."[1]

We must remain consciously aware of and guard our mouths, as a mother would stand guard over her baby. It takes that kind of commitment and dedication on our part. I have found that if I talk less and listen more, I will be less likely to sin with my tongue. Watching our words takes practice. Some people say, "Well, I just say whatever comes to mind. I speak my piece." Well, that is a lack of self-control and immaturity. James 1:26 says, "If any man among you seem to be religious, and bridleth not his tongue, but deceiveth his own heart, this man's religion is vain." We are to bridle our tongue, or we are deceived. Proverbs 29:20 states, "Seest thou a man that is hasty in his words? there is more hope of a fool than of him."

James gives us a clue just how we are to accomplish this. In James 3:13 he says, "Who is a wise man and endued with knowledge among you? Let him shew out of a good conversation his works with meekness of wisdom." In other words, if we live a consistent life of works for the Lord, speak of the good things of God in meekness, and show wisdom in what we do, it will help us in our conversation to keep it godly. If we meditate on His Word *all the day*, as David did (Ps. 119:97), we won't give our mouths an opportunity to sin. Psalm 119:131, 172 says, "I opened my mouth and panted: for I longed for thy commandments....My tongue shall speak of thy word." Psalm 71:24 says, "My tongue shall talk of thy righteousness all the day long." That is how we control the tongue.

Matthew Henry's Commentary on James 3:13, states, "If we are wiser than others, this should be evidenced by the goodness of our conversation, not by roughness or vanity of it. Words that inform, and heal, and do good, are the marks of wisdom.... True wisdom may be known by its works. The conversation here does not refer only to words, but to the whole of men's practice; therefore it is said, let him show out of a good conversation his works."[2]

The tongue can speak great things, but the Bible is full of warnings and of the potential damage it can cause. Because most men cannot control it, the negative is mostly emphasized and warned about throughout the Bible. However, there are verses on the positive that show us what we are to do with our tongues:

> My tongue shall speak of thy righteousness.
>
> —PSALM 35:28

> My tongue shall talk of thy righteousness all the day long.
>
> —PSALM 71:24

> I will speak of thy testimonies also before kings, and will not be ashamed.
>
> —PSALM 119:46

See more here: Psalms 45:1; 119:72, 131, 171; 126:2; Proverbs 25:11.

There are many verses I list ahead that show the great blessings that come to those who teach their mouths and control their tongues. Our tongues do have the ability to speak great things, if we would discipline ourselves to guard them. An extremely admirable attribute in someone is their ability to control their tongue. When we are angry, then that becomes the real test. Ephesians 4:26 says, "Be ye angry, and sin not." Our anger can really cause our mouths to get out of control.

True wisdom may be known by the meekness of the spirit and temper....It is a great instance of wisdom prudently to bridle our own anger, and patiently to bear the anger of others.[3]

To bridle our anger shows great wisdom. Laurence J. Peter said, "Speak when you're angry, and you will make the best speech you'll ever regret."[4]

Scriptures Regarding the Mouth

Look at these verses and see how important the tongue is:

- 1 Samuel 2:3—"Let not arrogancy come out of your mouth."

- Job 6:24–25—"Teach me, and I will hold my tongue: and cause me to understand where I have erred. How forcible are right words!"

- Job 19:2—"How long will ye vex my soul, and break me in pieces with words?"

- Psalm 12:3—"The LORD shall cut off all flattering lips."

- Psalm 17:4—"By the word of thy lips I have kept me from the paths of the destroyer."

- Psalm 50:23—"To him that ordereth his conversation aright will I shew the salvation of God."

- Proverbs 4:24—"Put away from thee a froward mouth, and perverse lips put far from thee."

- Proverbs 10:11—"Violence covereth the mouth of the wicked."

- Proverbs 10:14—"The mouth of the foolish is near destruction."

- Proverbs 10:19—"He that refraineth his lips is wise."

- Proverbs 10:31—"The froward tongue shall be cut out."

- Proverbs 12:14—"A man shall be satisfied with good by the fruit of his mouth."

- Proverbs 12:18—"The tongue of the wise is health."

- Proverbs 16:23—"The heart of the wise teacheth his mouth, and addeth learning to his lips."

- Proverbs 18:8—"The words of a talebearer are as wounds, and they go down into the inner most parts of the belly."

- Proverbs 18:21—"Death and life are in the power of the tongue."

- Proverbs 21:23—"Whoso keepeth his mouth and his tongue keepeth his soul from troubles."

- Proverbs 30:32—"If thou hast thought evil, lay thine hand across thy mouth."

- Matthew 15:11—"Not that which goeth into the mouth defileth a man; but that which cometh out of the mouth, this defileth a man."

- Luke 1:20—"Thou shalt be dumb and not speak" (because he spoke negative).

- Ephesians 4:29—"Let no corrupt communication proceed out of your mouth."

- 1 Peter 3:10—"He that would love life, and see good days, let him refrain his tongue from evil."

These verses speak for themselves. It is clear that our own words can cause us to experience life or death.

One of the strongest passages in the Bible is Mark 11:23–24. It says, "For verily I say unto you, That whosoever shall say unto this mountain, Be thou removed, and be thou cast into the sea, and shall not doubt in his heart, but shall believe that those things which he saith shall come to pass; he shall have whatsoever he saith. Therefore I say unto you, What things soever ye desire, when ye pray, believe that ye receive them, and ye shall have them."

Norvel Hayes says, "Jesus said to me, 'Son, you have to teach the people to talk to mountains and to the devils. "Mountains" or problems are caused by devils, so talk to the mountains and the devils and tell them to get out.'"[5]

He goes on to explain that people haven't been taught to talk to their mountain or problem. We talk about them, but we don't talk to them. I know this may sound foreign to some, but Jesus is the one who told us to talk to mountains. He said we would have whatever we say. So if you have lack, then that is your mountain. Tell it to go. Yes, that's right. Jesus said to talk to it, not about it. Matthew 21:21 says, "If ye have faith, and doubt not … ye shall *say* unto this mountain, Be thou removed, and be thou cast into the sea; it shall be done" (emphasis added). Did you get that? It takes faith and no doubt and speaking to the problem. Not many teach this in churches, but it is truth, and it works. You can believe the words of Jesus, or you can choose to disbelieve them. If you have doubt, you won't speak to mountains. Romans 4:17 states He "calleth those things which be not as though they were."

Jesus said in Matthew 12:34–35, "For out of the abundance of the heart the mouth speaketh. A good man out of the good treasure of the heart bringeth forth good things." The only way good things can come forth from a man is by placing good things in his heart. If you watch evil or dark movies, associate with ungodly people, and listen to doubt and fear, you will not produce good things. We have to put the Word in our hearts. If we do, we will speak what He said about our succeeding and not our doubts. What we speak will make the difference whether we will succeed or not. Words are extremely important, as Jesus said in Matthew 12:36, "But I say unto you, That every idle word that men shall speak, they shall give account thereof in the day of judgment." Is that scary or what? Every idle word ever spoken! The word *idle* in *Strong's* is the Greek word *argos*. It means "lazy, useless, ineffective, careless." Do you think you might want to pay more attention to your words?

A True Story About the Power of Words

I had another friend, Bob, and his wife whom I used to associate with on a regular basis. We were good friends for years and worked at the same office together. They were also Christians. One day we were talking about words—the power of God's Word. I shared with him how I had been learning about the importance of guarding our mouths. In the Bible it states that you will receive whatever comes out of your mouth. Our sales training courses also taught that principle of speaking positive words. But the Bible takes it much further. If we not only speak positive words, but God's own words, it is much more powerful. You will truly get what you say, as Mark 11:23–24 states.

Well, I went on to show Bob all the verses I had been writing down in regard to your mouth. I had over three hundred of them. Well, Bob was one who would always joke about himself in a negative way. He would say things like, "I'm so broke I can't pay attention." Or, "If I wash my car, you can be sure it will rain." Or, "I look at food and gain weight." Or, "If I have any luck at all, it will be bad." They were things of that nature. Now I know it can be all in jest, but it is actually not good to say negative things about yourself, even if it's all in fun. Ephesians 5:3-4 says, "Let it not be once named among you...nor foolish talking, nor jesting." This principle in the Bible regarding receiving what we say really does work, whether in the positive or in the negative.

Well, he suddenly got angry with me and didn't want to hear it. He wouldn't even read the verses. I wondered why, since we were friends and could talk about anything. He actually said, "I don't believe those verses mean that you get what you say. They don't mean that." I was surprised. All I asked is that he read them, but he refused. Keep in mind; he is a Christian. It's not as though he were hostile to the Bible. He just didn't like the teaching that tells us that we get what we say, even though the Bible is filled with verses on it.

Well, surprisingly, that small incident damaged our friendship. After a while, they ended up moving to another state, and I didn't hear from them for ten years. I was saddened that it would anger them to the point of no contact for so long. One day, I received a call from Bob. I was surprised to get the call. We caught up on our lives, and then he started to tell me about a dream he had that totally changed his life. I asked him to please tell me. He said that in the dream he was driving down the highway, and suddenly his windshield was being bombarded with "words" hitting the glass. There were thousands of words drifting in the air, and as he was moving along, they would all collide with the car. He said he asked God for the interpretation. God told him, not in an audible voice but in an inner voice, that the words were his negative words he spoke every day, crashing into his life and causing damage. His life had gone downhill for years. God wanted him to see how important words were and that he had greatly hindered his life with words that were contrary to God's words. He would need to learn to speak what God said about himself and no longer say the negative. He would need to reverse what he had put into action for so many years. I was happy that he finally saw the truth of the power of God's Word.

Now back to the time they moved away, which was ten years earlier. I had felt to pray and fast for him. I knew there was a stronghold over his mind. I fasted for ten days, water only. It is interesting it took ten years. But God answered my prayer for him. The point is this: the Word is powerful, and even if you don't believe it, words are working in your life one way or the other. Whatever your world is now, it is because you spoke it.

> Ye…break me in pieces with words.
>
> —JOB 19:2

> A man shall be satisfied with good by the fruit of his mouth.
>
> —PROVERBS 12:14

> Death and life are in the power of the tongue.
>
> —PROVERBS 18:21

> Whoso keeps his mouth and his tongue keepeth his soul from troubles.
>
> —PROVERBS 21:23

> If thou hast thought evil, lay thine hand across thy mouth.
>
> —PROVERBS 30:32

Your words have been stout against me.

—MALACHI 3:13

Not that which goeth into the mouth defileth a man;
but that which cometh out of the mouth, this defileth a man.

—MATTHEW 15:11

Keeping Your Word Sometimes Costs

I had my own home for sale, and this one particular day there
were two real estate agents who brought potential buyers to view
it. They both left, and about an hour later I received a call from
one of them. She said she had an offer and asked if she could come
by and present it. She came over, and the offer was twenty thousand dollars less than my asking price. I refused it and felt not to
counter it at this point. She called back later and asked if I would
consider taking five thousand dollars less than my asking price. I
told her I would, so she was going to put it in writing and would
be back for me to sign in about two hours.

Well, after we hung up, I received a call from the other agent
who told me she had an offer of five thousand dollars over the
asking price, and it was all cash. Now I thought, "What do I do?"
I hadn't signed anything with the other agent, but I told her I
would, and she was on her way.

Now I know I wasn't obligated to go ahead with her, as it
must be in writing to be binding, but I gave my word. The second
offer was ten thousand dollars more, so I was very tempted to
simply say no to the first, especially since the second offer was
all cash. I just couldn't find peace about taking the higher offer,
because of my word given. That might sound a little overboard,
because I would not be doing anything unethical by taking the

higher one. To make a long story short, I took the lower offer. The second agent couldn't believe I would pass on the higher offer. I explained to her that I was very strong about keeping my word, even if I didn't have to.

She couldn't get over that I would do that and lose ten grand. I told her I was a Christian, and as Christians we should value our words and honor them. She said she was not a Christian and met many who didn't keep their word.

Well, fifteen years later, I walked into a restaurant and ran into a pastor friend whom I hadn't seen for quite some time. He was there with four others. This one particular woman in the group with him asked if I was Bill Wiese. I said, "Yes, I am."

She said, "You are the real estate agent who was selling his own home and turned down ten thousand dollars extra in order to keep your word."

I said, "Yes, and I'm surprised you would remember me."

She said, "Well, what you don't know is, after I left your house that night, I met a girlfriend for dinner. During the evening we began discussing Christianity, because she was a Christian. She was telling me that the Bible teaches that a person should always keep their word. I told her that I had met a Christian like that tonight who kept his word in spite of a loss of ten thousand dollars. Well, she ended up leading me in a prayer to accept the Lord as my Savior that very night. I was so impressed at the commitment you had in keeping your word that it helped influence me to make that decision."

Even though it seemed foolish at the time to turn down the agent's higher price, I couldn't have known that it would influence her to something far more important, such as the saving of her eternal soul. What are the chances of my running into her fifteen years later and her recognizing me? I believe God wanted me to learn that sometimes we may not fully understand why we feel led to do a certain thing but to always be sensitive to the voice of God to direct us. Her soul was far more valuable than the ten thousand dollars. Psalm 49:8 says, "For the redemption of their soul is precious."

As for our words being important, virtually every sales training class for real estate that I attended stressed the careful choosing of your words. They would explain how important it is to speak positive over your life. This is not only coming from Christians but also from the world. John C. Maxwell quotes Emile de Girardin as saying, "The power of words is immense. A well-chosen word has often sufficed to stop a flying army, to change defeat into victory, and to save an empire."[6]

Sometimes our mind-sets can cause us to dismiss even the truth. God has placed different teachers in the body of Christ to equip us. No one has it all, as we all need the piece that has been revealed to the other. If we remain teachable, we can become the beneficiaries of some of the great teachings that are available today throughout the body of Christ.

Our tongue is so powerful, and if we can learn to use it to speak God's Word, instead of doubt, unbelief, fear, lack, and the negative we pick up from the world, we will live a blessed life. Our own mouths set the boundaries for our life. These are all ingredients it takes to make us well-developed and mature Christians. It is a lifelong process. Are you willing to learn? If you are, then you can't help but prosper. It doesn't matter what the economy is doing, because you would no longer be operating in only this earthly system. God's ways work all the time and can never fail. The world's system is failing in every area. There is no stability in anything. There is only one thing that is stable, and that is Jesus Christ. His Word will never pass away (Matt. 24:35).

He also said in Isaiah 55:11, "So shall my word be that goeth forth out of my mouth: it shall not return unto me void, but it shall accomplish that which I please, and it shall prosper in the thing whereto I sent it." God can never change His Word or alter it (Ps. 89:34; 119:89; Eccles. 3:14). Once He has spoken, it stands forever. And He made us in His image. We are to operate and value our words as He does and as He commands us.

Guarding our mouths is a big challenge, but if we will practice it, we will prosper. Adhering to God's ways will always cause us to prosper. This is why I can proclaim boldly that this is the only way we can have recession-proof living.

CHAPTER 19

THE BOTTOM LINE–A SYNOPSIS

IF WE LIVE godly, we will have success during any economic period. Here is a summary as to what we are to do in order to prosper. If we do these things, we will never fail or have shortage.

1. **Seek after wisdom**. Proverbs 3:13–16 states, "Happy is the man that findeth wisdom, and the man that getteth understanding....Length of days is in her right hand; and in her left hand riches and honour." This is a promise that is not dependent on our economic system. The key to receiving this godly wisdom is you must first know Him and fear Him (Prov. 9:10). Another way to gain wisdom is to be a soulwinner (Prov. 11:30).

2. **Seek first the kingdom of God** (Matt. 6:33). This is essential in order for us to prosper. I mentioned what "seeking the kingdom" entails in chapter 12. If we do, "all things shall be added" unto us.

3. **Pray and read the Word.** Joshua 1:8 says, "This book of the law shall not depart out of thy mouth, but thou shalt meditate…observe to do…then thou shalt make thy way prosperous…and have good success." (See also Deuteronomy 6:1–9; 28:1–14; 30:1–19; Proverbs 3:1–3.) We are to worship Him and pray daily (Ps. 29:2; 45:11; 95:6; Matt. 4:10; John 4:23).

4. **Tithe** (Mal. 3:10–11). This is the only place in the Bible where God tells us to test Him. If we trust Him with our tithes, He will "pour you out a blessing, that there shall not be room enough to receive it." He goes on to say, "And I will rebuke the devourer for your sakes, and he shall not destroy the fruits of your ground." That means nothing will be stolen from you. That is a promise from God. Proverbs 3:9–10, "Honor the LORD with thy substance, and with the fruits of all thine increase. So shall thy barns be filled with plenty."

5. **Feed the poor.** Proverbs 28:27 states, "He that giveth unto the poor shall not lack." Then Luke 6:38 says, "Give, and it shall be given unto you; good measure, pressed down, and shaken together, and running over, shall men give into your bosom."

6. **Honor your parents**, "which is the first commandment with promise; that it may be *well with thee, and thou mayest live long on the earth*" (Eph. 6:2–3, emphasis added). Another promise!

7. **Fast.** In Isaiah 58, God says what He will do for the one who fasts and deals his bread to the hungry. He says, "Thine health shall spring forth speedily...the glory of the Lord shall be thy reward [protection]...then shalt thou call, and the Lord shall answer....He shall say, Here I am....And the Lord shall guide thee continually, and satisfy thy soul in drought, and make fat thy bones: and thou shalt be like a watered garden" (vv. 8–11). How's that for a promise? Notice it says we will be satisfied in drought. *That means during a recession.* Psalm 37:19 says, "In the days of famine, they shall be satisfied." (See also Isaiah 58:6–7; Matthew 6:16; Acts 10:30; 13:2–3; 14:23; 1 Corinthians 7:5.)

8. **Lay up for yourself treasures in heaven**. Jesus said in Matthew 6:19–21, "Lay not up for yourselves treasures upon earth, where moth and rust doth corrupt, and where thieves break through and steal: But lay up for yourselves treasures in heaven, where neither moth nor rust doth corrupt, and where thieves do not break through nor steal: For where your treasure is, there will your heart be also." This is the only place where we have a 100 percent guarantee of no loss on our investment and also of increase. In Mark 10:29–30, Jesus said if any man leave his house, brother or sister, father or mother, wife or children, or lands for His sake,

that he shall receive a hundredfold return in this life. This is a promise with one hundred times the return on your investment.

9. **Be humble**. Proverbs 22:4 says, "By humility and the fear of the LORD are riches, and honour, and life." This is one of the most important keys in the Bible. If anyone will walk in humility and the fear of the Lord, they will always succeed.

10. **Obey God**. Job 36:11 says, "If they obey and serve him, they shall spend their days in prosperity, and their years in pleasures." Isaiah 1:19 says, "If ye be willing and obedient, ye shall eat the good of the land." (See also Deuteronomy 8:18; 28:1–13; Joshua 1:8; Proverbs 3:9–10.) One of the most fundamental things we are to do as Christians is to witness and share the gospel. Proverbs 11:30 says, "He that winneth souls is wise." This is our calling, and if we do not, God will hold us accountable. (See also Ezekiel 33:8; Matthew 24:14; Mark 1:15; 16:15; Acts 18:6; 20:26; Colossians 1:28.) Included in obedience is also to be thankful to the Lord. Coming to Him in thanksgiving and expressing it daily is what we are to do as Christians: "In every thing give thanks: for this is the will of God in Christ Jesus concerning you" (1 Thess. 5:18). Giving thanks is another thing that pleases God (Ps. 30:12; 100:4; 107:1; 2 Cor. 2:14; Col. 3:17; 2 Thess. 2:13).

11. **Show God your faith**. In Hebrews 11:6 we learn that "without faith it is impossible to please him....He is a rewarder of them that diligently seek him." First John 3:22 says, "Whatsoever we ask

we receive of him, because we keep his commandments, and do those things that are pleasing in his
sight." If we have faith, it pleases Him because our
faith and trust in Him are considered as righteousness. Righteousness is what is needed in order for
God to bless us. He is not pleased if He cannot
bless us. "Whatsoever we ask we receive," because
we please Him by trusting His Word and obeying
Him. "Whatsoever" covers a lot!

12. **Get an understanding of grace.** Second
    Corinthians 9:8 says, "And God is able to make
    all grace abound toward you; that ye, always
    having *all sufficiency in all things*" (emphasis
    added). We understand that it is by His grace and
    not by our works that we can obtain the blessings
    He has for us (Eph. 2:8–9; 4:7; Col. 1:6; 1 Tim. 1:14;
    2 Tim. 2:1).

13. **Understand the fear of the Lord.** Proverbs 19:23,
    "The fear of the Lord tendeth to life; and he that
    hath it shall *abide satisfied*; he shall *not be visited
    with evil*" (emphasis added). If we fear Him, we will
    obey Him. (See Deuteronomy 17:19; Psalm 2:11; 33:8;
    64:9; Proverbs 2:5; 16:6; Matthew 10:28; Acts 2:43.)

14. **Pray for Jerusalem.** Support Israel in prayer,
    finances, and love. When you do that, you will
    prosper. Psalm 122:6 says, "Pray for the peace
    of Jerusalem: they shall prosper that love thee."
    Genesis 12:3 says, "And I will bless them that bless
    thee, and curse him that curseth thee." Isaiah
    66:10–14 says, "Rejoice ye with Jerusalem…and
    your bones shall flourish." If you support Israel,

pray for Jerusalem, and rejoice for her, you will most certainly be blessed. (See also Genesis 13:2, 6; 15:14, 18; 17:2; 22:17–18; 24:35; 26:4.)

15. **Express God's love.** First Corinthians 13:8 says, "Love never fails" (NKJV). That is amazing. If we operate in God's love, we can never fail. That is a solid guarantee for success. Showing people real love goes further than anything else. Placing their needs ahead of yours, feeding the poor, showing consideration, being kind, and being honest is what showing love means. Being quick to forgive and quick to repent is a major key in showing love to others and obedience to God. You will have favor with them, they will trust you, and you will never fail. (See John 15:9; 17:23, 26; Ephesians 2:4; 1 John 2:10; 4:7–10; Revelation 1:5.)

God will deliver those who will trust in Him out of all evil. Look at these verses:

> This poor man cried, and the LORD heard him, and saved him out of all his troubles.
> —PSALM 34:6

> For he hath delivered me out of all trouble.
> —PSALM 54:7

> The LORD shall preserve thee from all evil.
> —PSALM 121:7

> The blessing of the LORD, it maketh rich, and he addeth no sorrow with it.
> —PROVERBS 10:22

The righteous is delivered out of all trouble.

—PROVERBS 11:8

The fear of the LORD tendeth to life: and he that hath it shall abide satisfied; he shall not be visited with evil.

—PROVERBS 19:23

Whoso keepeth the commandments shall feel no evil thing.

—ECCLESIASTES 8:5

And delivered him out of all his afflictions.

—ACTS 7:10

Persecutions, afflictions…but out of them all the Lord delivered me.

—2 TIMOTHY 3:11

These are promises that God has for all who will believe Him and obey Him. He has done this for me for over forty years and has never let me down, not even once. You can be delivered out of any and all problems, no matter how serious. His Word works, all the time, in any market, and in any condition.

Keep therefore the words of this covenant, and do them, that ye may prosper in all that ye do.

—DEUTERONOMY 29:9

CHAPTER 20

THE GOD MANY DON'T KNOW

THERE ARE THOSE who may see God as someone who restricts their life, takes away their freedom, and isn't really concerned about them personally. They may have never really read the Bible and yet have the opinion that it is boring and not relevant to today's society. Yet, quite the contrary, as the Bible teaches us how to get to know this God we serve, how to avoid the pitfalls of life, and how to receive His blessings.

God is not trying to restrict our lives but to protect our lives. His reason for warning us is so that we can escape the evil that would come upon us. There are spiritual laws that are in motion, just as there are physical laws. We wouldn't expect to step off a rooftop and just float down to the ground, would we? No, because of the law of gravity being in effect. In the same way, there are spiritual laws in effect, such as the law of sin and death (Rom. 8:2). In this law, evil pursues sinners (Prov. 13:21). It hunts the violent man down to overthrow him (Ps. 140:11). If someone lives in sin, evil will be attracted to them as metal is to a magnet. You cannot get away with sin, and that is why God warns us to not participate in it. It is for our own good, just as a parent would warn a child not to stick a fork into an electrical socket. We shouldn't get offended by these warnings but rather embrace them. His desire is to bless us, and that can come only through our obedience.

For many, to serve and obey anyone comes across with a negative connotation akin to slavery and tyranny! To them, God looks mean and unfair and ready to hit them over the head the moment they displease Him. Yet they don't realize that the reason God wants us to obey and serve Him is so He can protect us from harm. As a result of their misinformed view, they may steer clear of anything to do with God, church, or Christians. Because of their damaged souls, they refuse God's love and reject Him.

Others have received a twisted view of God from religion. Religion represents the father whose approval you strive for but will never receive. You are never "good" enough to receive God's love and acceptance. Religion teaches you to keep countless rules, but you never know why. You also never know God personally, and He really doesn't sound like someone you'd want to spend time with because He is too demanding. However, that is not the God of the Bible. He has been extremely misrepresented over the centuries. No, God is not mean, and He has provided a plan for our lives and a way for us to live with Him in heaven.

Mike Bickle states, "As a young Christian I had a certain zeal to discipline myself to gain spiritual ground so that I could earn

God's affection and favor. When I succeeded, I became spiritually proud. When I failed, I felt condemned. Eventually, I recognized that, like the Pharisees of old, I was trying to earn God's favor by my spiritual disciplines and achievements." He goes on to say how the enemy constructs a stronghold in our minds starting with lies about the personality of God. Bickle says, "Satan erects every stronghold he can to keep us from the true knowledge of God....Our ideas often come from our relationships with earthly authority figures."[1]

He explains that some have a father who is passive, authoritative, abusive, absent, accusatory, or one who ridiculed them. They may view God as such and go through their lives not wanting anything to do with Him.

Another reason people have a twisted view of God is because of evil that occurs on the earth. They think, "Where was God when that occurred?" But what they do not realize is not everything that happens on the earth is the will of God. As a matter of fact, most things are not His will at all. Jesus said to pray that God's will would be done on the earth (Matt. 6:10). Many do not pray, so His will is not done.

You might be thinking, "What about God's sovereignty?" Yes, God is sovereign, but only outside of His established Word. In other words, He will not do anything against what He has already written. His Word is forever settled in heaven, and He cannot alter the thing that has gone out of His mouth (Ps. 89:34; 119:89). If it is spelled out in His Word, then we know what His will is for that particular thing. For instance, we know it is His will for all to be saved (John 1:29; 6:40, 47, 51; Rom. 10:13; 2 Cor. 5:19; 1 Tim. 2:4–6; Heb. 2:9; 2 Pet. 3:9). He would not ever say that this one or that one can't be saved. No, since the Scripture is clear about it. But if it is not spelled out, then He is, of course, sovereign.

Understanding, Knowing, and Obeying God's Word

In addition, God holds us accountable to know what is written. Ephesians 5:17 states, "Wherefore be ye not unwise, but understanding what the will of the Lord is."

What about when Jesus came near to the city of Jerusalem and wept, saying, "If you hadst known...the time of thy visitation" (Luke 19:42, 44). They were held accountable to know the Scriptures (Heb. 10:7), which told of His day to enter Jerusalem as the Savior of the world (Ps. 118:21–24; Isa. 25:8–9; Zech. 9:9).

Also, when the disciples could not cast out a devil in Matthew 17, Jesus said, "O faithless and perverse generation, how long shall I be with you?" (v. 17). He expected them to know how to deal with the demon and to have the faith required to cast it out.

When Jesus was talking to His disciples about the suffering He would soon endure, Peter rebuked Him, saying, "This shall not be unto thee" (Matt. 16:22). Jesus responded with, "Get thee behind me, Satan." Jesus didn't say, "Well, that's all right, Peter; I know you meant well." No, He rebuked him because he should have known the scriptures regarding His suffering and dying. (See Psalms 22; 34:20; 41:9; Isaiah 7:14; 50:6; 53:5; Hosea 11:1; Amos 8:9; Micah 5:2; Zechariah 9:9.)

Jesus was very direct when it came to His Word. God wants us well and prosperous in order to enjoy life and to be able to help others. He also said if you leave or give up homes, or land, or family for the gospel's sake, you would receive a hundredfold return in this life (Mark 10:30). You can't out give God.

Now, if we disobey Him over and over, He will take His hand

of protection and blessing off of us (Deut. 31:17–18). He also will allow the devil to come in and destroy someone in order for them to be saved. In 1 Corinthians 5:5 it states, "To deliver such an one unto Satan for the destruction of the flesh, that the spirit may be saved." God will allow sickness or poverty to come on someone, but it is only if they are rebellious to His Word and ignore His repeated warnings (Deut. 8:19–20; 28:27–28, 35, 59–61, 66; Job 33:19–20). Those verses are absolutely clear. God is not the one making people sick or broke, especially His children (John 10:10).

Just as a side note: not all people are His children. John 17:9 says, "I pray for them [those that have kept thy word (v. 6)]: I pray not for the world, but for them which thou hast given me; for they are thine." Galatians 3:26 states, "For ye are all the children of God by faith in Christ Jesus." (See also John 1:12; 8:44; Romans 9:7–8; Ephesians 5:1; 1 Peter 1:14.)

God's Love Saves Our Souls

God loves us, and He is the one who provided healing and provision on the cross. In 2 Corinthians 8:9 it states, "He became poor, that ye through his poverty might be rich." All through the Bible God promises long, healthy, and prosperous lives to those who obey (Gen. 12:2; 15:18; 17:6–9; 18:18; 22:17–18; 24:35; Deut. 28; 3 John 2).

God wants us to learn through His Word. In Psalm 32:8 it states that God will guide them with His eye. Remember when you were a child and your parents just gave you "the eye" if you got out of line? That is how God wants us to learn, to be sensitive to His correction, and not like one who has to have the bit in his mouth as it says in James 3:3. "Be ye not as the horse, or as the mule," it says in Psalm 32:9, "which have no understanding: whose mouth must be held in with bit and bridle, lest they come near unto thee." If we remain teachable, we can learn the easy way (Ps. 119:14, 20, 47).

This earthly prosperity is meaningless without our soul being saved. To achieve great wealth and even enjoy a healthy life is but nothing when compared to the destination of our eternal soul. Jesus said in Matthew 16:26, "For what is a man profited, if he shall gain the whole world, and lose his own soul? or what shall a man give in exchange for his soul?" Psalm 49:8–9 says it this way: "For a soul is far too precious to be ransomed by mere earthly wealth. There is not enough of it in all the earth to buy eternal life for just one soul, to keep it out of hell" (TLB). In Proverbs 27:12, King Solomon said, "A prudent man foreseeth the evil, and hideth himself; but the simple pass on and are punished."

Everyone who doesn't call on Jesus as their Savior should ask themselves these questions:

- If there is no God, then there would be no consequences for our actions. Would that be just?

- If there is no hell, then there would never be any justice served. Would that be fair?

- If there is a heaven, then are we simply entitled to go to this perfect place?

- Do we really think we're "good enough," if even our thoughts and motives are examined?

- Why should God allow us into heaven?

If you are not positive about the answers to these questions, then are you really willing to risk your eternal soul on simply your opinion? It should be based on something more concrete. The Bible is the only secure foundation to stand on.

Most people would agree that they would desire to go to heaven. Well then, shouldn't they find out how to get there from the One who created it? His directions for us to go there should be more valued than simply your opinion, right? Another point many people do not realize is that all of us, above the age of accountability, are automatically on the road to hell because of sin (Ps. 51:1–5; 58:3; John 3:17–18). God is not sending people to hell; they are already automatically going there. That is why Jesus came and died for us, to get us off that road.

Jesus dealt with our sin on the cross, and God took out His anger on Jesus for our sake. But if someone refuses to trust in Jesus for salvation, then they will have to endure the punishment. Our part is to simply show some humility and ask for forgiveness. He will forgive us completely and remember our sins no more (Ps. 103:11–12; Heb. 8:12; 10:17). We just come as we are; we do not need to clean up our act first.

However, because He loves us, He has given us a free will to choose. (See John 1:29; 6:40, 51; Romans 10:13; 1 Timothy 2:4–6; 2 Peter 3:9.) Do you believe His words or not? Jesus said in Matthew 12:37, "For by thy words thou shalt be justified, and by thy words thou shalt be condemned." Your own words will determine where you spend eternity. If you say, "Well, I don't believe the Bible," well, just know that Revelation 21:8 states that all unbelievers shall have their part in the lake of fire. He just told us where we will go if we don't believe Him. So it is our choice.

God has a book, and on Judgment Day He will look to see if your name is in His book (Rev. 20:15). The worst words you could ever hear would be Him saying, "Depart from me, ye cursed, into everlasting fire, prepared for the devil and his angels" (Matt. 25:41). That is what He will have to say to anyone who denies Him as their Lord and Savior (Luke 13:3; John 3:36; Acts 4:12; 1 John 5:12). This decision is final. There is no second chance, no turning back, no friend to turn to, and no appeals court. One second after you die it's too late. This decision needs to be made now, while you have the opportunity. We all must repent (Luke 13:3; Acts 17:30; 26:20), which means to turn away from our sin and to feel remorse for our sins (2 Cor. 7:9). We must confess Him as Lord and Savior and invite Him into our hearts (Rom. 10:9–10).

So my question for you is this: Do you know if your name is written in His book? You must be certain on this one. If you have any doubt, then you need to say this prayer and make this commitment to Him:

> *Dear God in heaven, I know that I am a sinner, and I cannot save myself. I believe You sent Your Son Jesus to die in my place. I believe He died, was buried, and rose again, and lives forevermore. I ask You to forgive me of my sins. I repent, and I turn away from sin. I want to follow You all the days of my life. It is not my good works that save me, but the shedding of Your blood that washes away my sins. I ask You to come into my heart. I receive You as my Lord and Savior. You are the Son of God. And I thank You, Jesus, for saving me from hell and for taking me to heaven with You. I believe I am now a born-again Christian and going to heaven. In Jesus's name I pray, amen.*

For further study, read: Psalms 9:17; 30:3; 40:2; 86:13; Isaiah 38:17; Matthew 13:41; 18:8; 24:51; Mark 9:47; Luke 16:23; John 3:36; Romans 3:23; 6:23; 10:9–10; 1 Corinthians 15:3–4; 2 Thessalonians 1:8–9.

Now that you are saved, there are four very important things for you to do.

1. Read the Bible daily. This is not a religious exercise, but it will teach you how to get to know this wonderful God we serve, how to keep you away from the pitfalls of the enemy, and how to obtain the blessings He has for you.

2. Get involved in a Bible-teaching church, and attend regularly. You will grow going to church.

3. Associate with godly people.

4. We are instructed in the Word to get water baptized. This is simply showing an outward sign of an inward commitment. It represents death to our old nature and resurrection to this new life in Christ. "Baptism is connected with death and burial in the N.T., not with spiritual birth...it mentions Baptism as the expected outward expression of belief. Baptism is not a condition of salvation, but an outward proclamation that the person has been saved."[2] (For further study to see that baptism is not a "requirement" for salvation, but should still be done, there are thirty-three verses which state to repent, that your sins be blotted out [Acts 3:19], and don't mention baptism. Only four verses mention it. Also, one hundred fifty verses state that salvation is by faith alone. The thief on the cross was saved and not baptized—Acts 10:44–48 makes this absolutely clear.) If baptism was a requirement for salvation, then Romans 10:13 and John 6:40 wouldn't work, and God could never

save someone in a deathbed experience, a plane
crash, a foxhole, or any other crisis situation. God
is certainly not limited in His ability to save.

This is just the beginning. As you read His Word, you will
acquire a desire to serve Him. His desire is to bless you as you are
obedient to His Word (Matt. 6:33; Luke 11:10; 12:32). You, in turn,
will be able to help and bless others.

Thank you so very much for taking your time to read this book
and especially for your commitment to our Lord Jesus the Savior.
Stay strong in Him, obey Him, and you will have a blessed life.

ADDITIONAL VERSES: A PILOT'S CHECKLIST

❑ Deuteronomy 25:15—"But thou shalt have a perfect and just weight, a perfect and just measure shalt thou have: that thy days may be lengthened." Deal fairly.

❑ Joshua 1:8—"This book of the law shall not depart out of thy mouth...then thou shalt make thy way prosperous, and then thou shalt have good success."

❑ 2 Chronicles 26:5—"As long as he sought the LORD, God made him to prosper."

❑ Job 10:15—"I am full of confusion; therefore see thou mine affliction." This is why many are sick: not having a knowledge of the Word leaves us in confusion, and we don't know whether it is the devil attacking us, the Lord teaching us, or just our own stupidity.

❑ Job 17:5—"He that speaketh flattery to his friends, even the eyes of his children shall fail." Eye problems because of our parents! Pray to cancel it.

❑ Job 20:11—"His bones are full of the sin of his youth."

❑ Job 36:11—"If they obey and serve him, they shall spend their days in prosperity, and their years in pleasures."

❑ Psalm 26:1—"I have walked in mine integrity: I have trusted also in the LORD; therefore I shall not slide."

❑ Psalm 31:24—"Be of good courage, and he shall strengthen your heart."

❑ Psalm 32:3—"When I kept silence my bones waxed old."

❑ Psalm 37:21—"The wicked borroweth, and payeth not again."

❑ Psalm 54:7—"He hath delivered me from all trouble."

❑ Psalm 62:10—"If riches increase, set not your heart upon them." Seek first the kingdom of God.

❑ Psalm 104:15—"Bread [spiritual and physical] which strengtheneth man's heart."

❑ Psalm 107:20—"He sent his word, and healed them, and delivered them from their destructions."

❑ Proverb 3:7–8—"Fear the LORD, and depart from evil. It shall be health to thy navel, and marrow to thy bones." Avoid evil and enjoy healthy bones.

❑ Proverbs 3:9–10—"Honour the LORD with thy substance, and with the firstfruits [tithe] of all thine increase: so shall thy barns be filled with plenty."

❑ Proverbs 3:27—"Withhold not good from them to whom it is due, when it is in the power of thine hand to do it."

❑ Proverbs 4:20–22—"Attend to my words; incline thine ear unto my sayings. Let them not depart from thine eyes; keep them in the midst of thine heart. For they are life unto those that find them, and health to all their flesh."

❑ Proverbs 4:23—"Keep thy heart with all diligence; for out of it are the issues of life." What are you allowing into your ear and eye gates? It all affects your heart.

❑ Proverbs 6:12–15—"A wicked man, walketh with a froward mouth. He winketh with his eyes.... Frowardness is in his heart, he deviseth mischief continually; he soweth discord. Therefore shall his calamity come suddenly; suddenly shall he be broken without remedy."

❑ Proverbs 10:4—"He becometh poor that dealeth with a slack hand." Be diligent.

❑ Proverbs 11:1—"A false balance is an abomination to the LORD." This is talking about our life balance.

❑ Proverbs 11:27—"He that diligently seeketh good procureth favour: but he that seeketh mischief, it shall come unto him."

❑ Proverbs 12:18—"The tongue of the wise is health." Watch your tongue.

❑ Proverbs 12:21—"There shall no evil happen to the just." Don't expect or voice it.

❑ Proverbs 13:10—"Only by pride cometh contention." Remain humble.

❑ Proverbs 13:18—"Poverty and shame shall be to him that refuseth instruction."

❑ Proverbs 15:30—"A good report maketh the bones fat." Healthy bones.

❑ Proverbs 16:24—"Pleasant words are as an honeycomb, sweet to the soul, and health to the bones.

❑ Proverbs 17:22—"A merry heart doeth good like a medicine." Be joyful.

❑ Proverbs 19:11—"The discretion of a man deferreth his anger; and it is his glory to pass over a transgression." Control your anger.

❑ Proverbs 19:23—"The fear of the LORD tendeth to life: and he that hath it shall abide satisfied. He shall not be visited with evil."

❑ Proverbs 21:17—"He that loveth pleasure shall be a poor man."

❑ Proverbs 21:23—"Whoso keepeth his mouth and his tongue keepeth his soul from troubles." Guard your mouth.

❑ Proverbs 22:7—"The rich ruleth over the poor, and the borrower is servant to the lender."

❑ Proverbs 22:16—"He that oppresseth the poor to increase riches, and he that giveth to the rich, shall surely come to want."

❑ Proverbs 23:4—"Labour not to be rich: cease from thine own wisdom." Rely on God's wisdom.

❑ Proverbs 23:21—"The drunkard and the glutton shall come to poverty."

❑ Proverbs 24:17—"Rejoice not when thine enemy falleth."

❑ Proverbs 24:25—"To them that rebuke him shall be delight, and a good blessing shall come upon them."

❑ Proverbs 24:33–34—"A little sleep...so shall thy poverty come as one that travelleth; and thy want as an armed man."

❑ Proverbs 28:10—"The upright shall have good things in possession."

❑ Proverbs 28:13—"He that covereth his sins shall not prosper."

❑ Proverbs 28:22—"He that hasteth to be rich hath an evil eye, and considereth not that poverty shall come upon him." This is talking about get-rich-quick schemes.

❑ Proverbs 29:5—"A man that flattereth his neighbour spreadeth a net for his feet."

❏ Ecclesiastes 5:4—"When thou vowest a vow unto God, defer not to pay it; for he hath no pleasure in fools."

❏ Jeremiah 5:4—"Surely these are poor; they are foolish: for they know not the way of the LORD."

❏ Jeremiah 5:25—"Your sins have withholden good things from you."

❏ Jeremiah 15:11—"I will cause the enemy to entreat thee well."

❏ Malachi 3:13–14—"Your words have been stout against me, saith the LORD.... Ye have said, It is vain to serve God: and what profit is it that we have kept his ordinance."

❏ Luke 8:39—"Shew how great things God hath done unto thee." Boast on God.

❏ Romans 12:11—"Not slothful in business." Work diligently.

❏ 1 Corinthians 16:14—"Let all your things be done with charity."

❏ 2 Corinthians 2:10–11—"Forgive any thing...lest Satan should get an advantage."

❏ 1 Thessalonians 5:14—"Be patient toward all men."

❏ 1 Thessalonians 5:22—"Abstain from all appearance of evil."

❏ 2 Timothy 2:24–25—"And the servant of the Lord must not strive; but be gentle unto all men, apt to teach, patient, in meekness instructing those that oppose themselves."

❏ Hebrews 11:6—"He is a rewarder of them that diligently seek him."

❏ James 5:16—"Pray one for another, that ye may be healed."

❏ 1 Peter 3:10—"For he that will love life, and see good days, let him refrain his tongue from evil, and his lips that they speak no guile."

ADDITIONAL VERSES: FEAR OF THE LORD

THERE IS A minimum of 243 verses regarding the fear of the Lord. Here are a few:

- Exodus 18:21—"Thou shalt provide out of all the people able men, such as fear God, men of truth, hating covetousness; and place such over them."

- Deuteronomy 17:19—"He shall read therein all the days of his life: that he may *learn to fear* the LORD his God, to *keep all the words of this law* and these statutes, to do them" (emphasis added).

- Psalm 2:11—"Serve the LORD with fear, and rejoice with trembling."

- Psalm 33:8—"Let all the earth fear the LORD."

- Psalm 34:11—"I will teach you the fear of the LORD."

- Psalm 64:9—"And all men shall fear, and shall declare the work of God; for they shall wisely consider of his doings."

- Psalm 89:7—"God is greatly to be feared in the assembly of the saints." Notice this is addressed to the church.

- Psalm 119:120, "My flesh trembleth for fear of thee."

- Proverbs 16:6—"By the fear of the LORD men depart from evil."

- Isaiah 66:2—"Saith the LORD: but to this man will I look, even to him that is poor and of a contrite spirit, and trembleth at my word."

- Jeremiah 5:22—"Fear ye not me? saith the LORD: will ye not tremble at my presence?"

- Jeremiah 32:40—"I will put my fear in their hearts, that they shall not depart from me."

- Daniel 6:26—"Men tremble and fear before the God of Daniel."

- Matthew 10:28—"Fear him which is able to destroy both soul and body in hell."

- Luke 5:26—When Jesus healed the paralyzed man, all were "filled with fear."

- Luke 7:16—When a boy was raised from the dead, "there came a fear on all."

- Luke 8:37—When the residents in the country of the Gadarenes urged Jesus to leave the area because the demon-possessed man had been miraculously delivered, it was because "they were taken with great fear."

- Acts 2:43—The Day of Pentecost was such that "fear came upon every soul."

- Acts 5:5—When Ananias was struck dead, "great fear came on all."

- Acts 9:31—"The churches...were edified; and walking in the fear of the Lord."

- Acts 19:17—When the sons of Sceva failed in their attempt to cast out demons but were overcome by them, the result was that "fear fell on them all, and the name of the Lord Jesus was magnified."

- Romans 11:20—"Be not highminded, but fear."

- Philippians 2:12—Paul said to "work out your own salvation with fear and trembling."

- 1 Timothy 5:20—Paul said, "Them that sin rebuke before all, that others also may fear."

- Hebrews 10:31—"It is a fearful thing to fall into the hands of the living God."

- Hebrews 11:7—Noah "moved with fear" in his obedience to God.

- Hebrews 12:28—"Let us have grace, whereby we may serve God acceptably with reverence and godly fear."

Further reading: Acts 5:11; 13:16; 2 Corinthians 7:1; Ephesians 5:21; Hebrews 12:21; 1 Peter 1:17; 2:17; Revelation 14:7.

NOTES

CHAPTER 6
TEN DOLLARS BUYS MORE THAN A HUNDRED
1. Phil Pringle, *Keys to Financial Excellence* (Dee Why, Australia: Pax Ministries Pty Ltd., 2003), 67.

CHAPTER 11
A PILOT'S CHECKLIST
1. Tommy Barnett, *Hidden Power* (Lake Mary, FL: Charisma House, 2002), 23–26.

2. John Bevere, *Driven by Eternity* (Nashville, TN: FaithWords, 2006), 126.

3. John Bevere, *The Fear of the Lord* (Lake Mary, FL: Charisma House), 91–92.

4. Bevere, *Driven by Eternity*, 91.

5. Andrew Wommack, *Grace, the Power of the Gospel* (Tulsa, OK: Harrison House Publishers, 2004), 71.

CHAPTER 12
ACTIVATE THE BLESSINGS IN GOD'S WORD
1. C. Thomas Anderson, *Becoming a Millionaire God's Way* (Nashville, TN: FaithWords, 2008), 30–31.

2. Theo Wolmarans, *How to Recognize the Voice of God* (Bonaero Park, S. Africa: Theo and Beverley Christian Enterprises, 2009), 165.

3. Edward K. Rowell, ed., *1001 Quotes, Illustrations and Humorous Stories* (Grand Rapids, MI: Baker Books, 2008), 42.

4. Jentezen Franklin, *Believe That You Can* (Lake Mary, FL: Charisma House, 2008), 46.

CHAPTER 13
PASSING THE TESTS OF LIFE
1. John Paul Jackson, *Needless Casualties of War* (n.p.: Streams Publications, 1999), 130–133.

2. Robert T. Kiyosaki, *Retire Young, Retire Rich* (n.p.: Business Plus, 2002), 5.

3. John C. Maxwell, *Failing Forward* (Nashville, TN: Thomas Nelson, 2007), 183.

4. Harold Myra and Marshall Shelley, *The Leadership Secrets of Billy Graham* (Grand Rapids, MI: Zondervan, 2005), 173.

5. Franklin, *Believe That You Can*, 116.

6. R. T. Kendall, *Out of Your Comfort Zone* (Nashville, TN: Faith-Words, 2006), 20, quoting Martin Luther.

7. Wolmarans, *How to Recognize the Voice of God*, 34–35.

CHAPTER 14
WISDOM—DO YOU HAVE IT?

1. Phil Pringle, *Leadership Excellence* (Dee Why, Australia: Pax Ministries Pty Ltd., 2005), 172.

2. Charles Spurgeon, *The Soul Winner* (New Kensington, PA: Whitaker House, 1995), 9.

3. Henry Cloud, *Necessary Endings* (New York: HarperBusiness, 2011).

4. Ibid.

5. Ibid.

6. Ibid.

CHAPTER 15
GOD'S WISDOM REVEALED

1. John MacArthur, *The MacArthur Bible Commentary* (Nashville, TN: Thomas Nelson, 2005), 1240, "Here it symbolizes Israel" (cf. Ps. 80:8–16; Isa. 5:1; Jer. 2:21).

2. John C. Maxwell, *There's No Such Thing as Business Ethics* (Nashville, TN: CenterStreet, 2003).

CHAPTER 16
THE POWER OF HUMILITY

1. Rowell, ed., *1001 Quotes, Illustrations and Humorous Stories*, 122.

2. Franklin, *Believe That You Can*, 80–82.

3. Pringle, *Leadership Excellence*, 189.

4. R. T. Kendall, *Imitating Christ* (Lake Mary, FL: Charisma House, 2007), 87–91.

5. Myra and Shelley, *The Leadership Secrets of Billy Graham*, 25.

CHAPTER 17
THE FEAR OF GOD

1. Bevere, *The Fear of the Lord*, 74.

2. Patrick Wiese, "Understanding God and Ways: God's Judicial Process," TrinityAssemblyLive.com, http://www.trinityassemblylive.com/Understanding_God_and_His_Ways.ihtml?id=644842 (accessed May 20, 2011).

3. Wayne Grudem, *Systematic Theology* (Grand Rapids, MI: Zondervan, 1994), 578.

4. Thomas Aquinas, *Summa Theologiae*, as quoted in Robert A. Peterson, *Hell on Trial* (Phillipsburg, NJ: Presbyterian and Reformed Publishing Co., 1995), 109.

5. Christopher W. Morgan and Robert A. Peterson, *Hell Under Fire* (Grand Rapids, MI: Zondervan, 2004), 210.

6. Kendall, *Out of Your Comfort Zone*, 64–67.

7. Bevere, *Driven by Eternity*, 90.

8. Bevere, *The Fear of the Lord*, 92.

9. Keith A. Butler, *A Seed Will Meet Any Need* (Tulsa, OK: Harrison House, 2002), 10–11.

10. Kendall, *Out of Your Comfort Zone*, 64–65.

11. William MacDonald, *Believer's Bible Commentary* (Nashville, TN: Thomas Nelson, 1989, 1990, 1992, 1995), 825.

12. Billy Graham, *The Classic Writings of Billy Graham* (n.p.: Inspirational Press, 2005), 196.

13. A. W. Tozer, *Jesus, Our Man in Glory* (n.p.: Wingspread Publishers, 2009), 22.

14. Charles Colson and Nancy Pearcey, *How Now Shall We Live?* (Carol Stream, IL: Tyndale House, 2005), 379.

15. C. S. Lewis, *The Lion, the Witch, and the Wardrobe* (New York: Harper Collins, 2010), Kindle e-book, chapter 8.

16. As quoted in Kendall, *Out of Your Comfort Zone*, 39.

17. Jack Hayford, *New Spirit-Filled Life Bible* (Nashville, TN: Thomas Nelson, 2002), 1147, s.v. "Hosea 3:5"; Strong's #6342.

CHAPTER 18
LIFE AND DEATH ARE WITHIN YOUR POWER

1. R. T. Kendall, *Controlling the Tongue* (Lake Mary, FL: Charisma House, 2007), 135–136.

2. Matthew Henry, *Matthew Henry's Commentary on the Whole Bible*, (n.p.: Hendrickson Publishers, 2005), 2415, s.v. "James 3:13".

3. Ibid.

4. Rowell, ed., *1001 Quotes, Illustrations and Humorous Stories*, 16.

5. Norvel Hayes, *How to Live and Not Die* (Tulsa, OK: Harrison House, 2005), 52.

6. John C. Maxwell, *The 360-Degree Leader* (Nashville, TN: Thomas Nelson, 2006), 91.

CHAPTER 20
THE GOD MANY DON'T KNOW

1. Mike Bickle, *Passion for Jesus* (Lake Mary, FL: Charisma House, 1993, 2007), 86–87.

2. MacDonald, *Believer's Bible Commentary*, 1364.

FOR FURTHER INFORMATION:

Bill & Annette Wiese
Soul Choice Ministries
P. O. Box 26588
Santa Ana, CA 92799

Website:

www.soulchoiceministries.com
www.23minutesinhell.com